My Dad Raced One of Those

THE JOYS OF CLASSIC MOTORSPORT

Alan Anderson

The History Press

Above: One-marque racing, run by owners' clubs, usually provides the easiest route into classic motorsport, with certain events also allowing road-legal cars to compete. (Silverstone Classic)

First published 2025

The History Press
97 St George's Place, Cheltenham,
Gloucestershire, GL50 3QB
www.thehistorypress.co.uk

British Library Cataloguing in Publication Data.
A catalogue record for this book is available from the British Library.

ISBN 978 1 80399 594 6

Typesetting and origination by The History Press
Printed in Turkey by IMAK

Front Cover: An Anglia 105E leading the pack at a typical classic car meeting. This fast Ford, along with forty-nine other legends, is highlighted in this book. (MagicCarPics)

Back Cover: A saloon car grid thrills the crowd at the Silverstone weekend. (Silverstone Classic.com)

FSC www.fsc.org MIX Paper from responsible sources FSC® C013056

Trees for Life

CONTENTS

Foreword by Gregor Marshall 5

Preface 8

A Brief History of the Evolution of British Motor Racing:
When the Flag Drops, the 'BS' Stops 9

Big Fun with a Midget by Terry Grimwood 19

All Good Sports 22

Cheap and Cheerful by Paul Davies 28

50 Racing Certs 31

God Made Man and Man Made the Capri by Holman Blackburn 138

Seasonal 140

Round-the-Clock Fun by Rex Greenslade 148

The Classic Scene 151

In it for the Long Haul by Barrie Carter 156

Acknowledgements 159

About the Author 160

Rallying requires a co-driver/navigator and is inherently harder on the car, which is something to bear in mind, especially if you cherish your Porsche 911! (Roger Albert Clark Rally)

FOREWORD

BY GREGOR MARSHALL

Growing up, I knew my late dad was a successful (as in winning) racing driver, but he was not necessarily famous. Yes, we would go to races every weekend and people would talk about him at the racetrack, but to me, someone was famous because they were on telly or talked about at school, not in racing magazines. One thing that did always interest me, however, was Dad had written two books and I knew he had also written columns for several magazines and occasionally still contributed to others – so he was nearly famous, I suppose! I was lucky to go racing with Dad every weekend and got to meet lots of famous racing drivers and, as I got older, I could see that the majority of them respected and even revered my father. And as I read more, I realised Dad had actually been famous. Every year he would sit me down at Christmas to watch the BBC's *100 Greatest Sporting Moments*, which included a 1971 race at Crystal Palace that Dad won, with the late Murray Walker going mad on the commentary!

I also got to see more of Dad's business, not just the car sales, but also the motor-racing team – I remember going to Gerry Marshall Racing at Silverstone, but more so to Marshall Asquith Racing in Croughton, and then at Dad's new garage in Tring when he moved from London. I read his biography, *Only Here for the Beer*; watched several Vauxhall and Castrol-produced videos; and just loved seeing his Baby Bertha and Old Nail racing cars together in the workshop, surrounded by racing Capris, Opel Monzas and rally Ford Escorts. It was then I knew that I wanted to become a racing driver. Dad's fame also became a little bit more recognised by me, as I got to meet several high-profile people that he had taught to race, people like Mark Thatcher

Legendary Gerry Marshall back in 1971 with what was affectionally known as 'Old Nail', which achieved more than sixty motorsport victories during its three years of competition. (Gregor Marshall)

(son of Maggie), Andrew Ridgeley (Wham), Luther Blissett (footballer), Lord (Charles) Brocket, Rowan Atkinson, Daley Thompson, and Falklands hero Simon Weston, to name a few.

Then the fateful day, 21 April 2005, happened. Dad/Gerry Marshall passed away while testing at Silverstone and I was devastated. He still owned his most famous and successful racing car, the 1971 Vauxhall Firenza – better known as 'Old Nail', which was currently on loan to Vauxhall at their Heritage Centre in Luton, before moving to the Donington Collection. This car, still going strong under a new owner, is etched in the fabric of British motor racing. I finally got the chance to drive Old Nail at Goodwood, the 2012 Festival of Speed, and to compete in a car that your father campaigned in is a unique experience as well as a privilege. So when I was approached to write a foreword to *My Dad Raced One of Those*, it certainly struck a chord. With classic motorsport ever increasing in popularity, there's not a better time for younger enthusiasts to compete in the same cars their fathers did and to enjoy the same simple thrills from a simpler time. This book looks at fifty of some of the most popular race and rally cars, from the 1950s to the mid-'90s, charting their success in the sport and how a similar car can be made competitive today. A brief look back on how motorsport evolved since the Second World War, its different categories, today's classic scene, and individual drivers' memories from the golden days of racing and rallying only adds to the fun reading.

I regularly look back at my days watching Dad race with great fondness, not least the joy it bought him, but also to the countless spectators, fans and marshals, and now as I also race my own 'Old Nail' replica it brings me closer to him; I'm sure it will do the same for you.

Gregor Marshall used to own his dad Gerry's actual Firenza racer, that he first drove back in 2012, but now has his own replica, which he displays and competes in. (Gregor Marshall/stellantis.com)

PREFACE

Anybody who has attended classic motorsport events, such as the Goodwood Revival, Silverstone Festival and Race Retro, will have come away enthralled and captivated by the sights, sounds and smells of retro racing and rallying. Before the millennium, motorsport was somehow so much simpler, cheaper, and more attainable and accessible, especially in the case of the amateur club scene. Perhaps that's why your dad decided to take up this all-engrossing hobby. *My Dad Raced One of Those* celebrates that golden era of motorsport; a time, indeed, where you could even compete successfully with the ordinary car you drove on a daily basis. This book highlights the history of grassroots British car competition from the Second World War up to the mid-1990s, and details all the major disciplines, such as racing, rallying, hill climbing, sprints and so on. Also, out of hundreds of potential cars eligible to participate over the decades, we pick out and celebrate our favourite fifty that made their mark in the sport – and often continue to do so – topped by a little-known factoid for each one.

A book like this wouldn't be complete without a look at what makes retro motorsport so popular today, and how you can follow in your parents' tyre tracks and enjoy the golden days of low-cost motorsport all over again.

A BRIEF HISTORY OF THE EVOLUTION OF BRITISH MOTOR RACING: WHEN THE FLAG DROPS, THE 'BS' STOPS

Henry Ford has been credited with the famous quip that the first ever motor race was conducted 'five minutes after the second car was built'. Ford only won a solitary motor race back in 1901 but, more importantly, it created enough interest around his fledgling company to help it get off the ground; the 'Blue Oval' has been associated with racing and rallying ever since. In the UK the first 'race' between two steam engines occurred on 30 August 1867 in Manchester, but the first official car race as we'd know it today was the Paris–Bordeaux–Paris event in 1895, which was won by a Peugeot.

This book concentrates on the history of motorsport in the UK since the end of the Second World War. By this time, Brands Hatch in Kent had become well established, while the ex-RAF base Silverstone held its first race in 1947. Circuits at Snetterton in Norfolk and Oulton Park in Cheshire were opened by the mid-1950s, and by then the sport really began to shape up, slowly evolving from a genial 'run what ya brung' (regularly a road-legal car) scene into competition between professional race and rally teams controlled and challenged by constantly changing regulations and modifications to the car so that they complied.

'Win on Sunday, sell on Monday' was becoming a popular catchphrase with carmakers, and an increasing number of manufacturers were getting in on the act. A typical race/rally starting grid would see a huge variety of entrants all mixing it, from tiny Austin A35s to big 200bhp Jaguar saloons (with nascent legends such as Stirling Moss and Britain's first F1 World Champion Mike

Hawthorn at the wheel). The watching crowds loved it: racegoers could relate to the makes and models on the track because they all looked pretty much like standard cars you could buy. Indeed, by and large they actually were! Modifications were rudimentary and standard car tyres, usually skinny cross-ply types, were used. Many events were essentially small-scale affairs run by keen regional motor clubs.

However, in 1958 the first British Racing & Sports Car Club (BRSCC) Saloon Car Championship was held and for the first time tightening regulations started to rear their authoritative heads. And the power stakes were really hotting up; for example, Jaguars could offer almost 300bhp, Ford Zephyrs could produce 170bhp, and even an Austin A35 could muster an easy 75bhp. The end of the 1950s saw a sea change in the sport. First, although it was classified as Formula Libre, regulations actually became far stricter. Second, giantkillers such as BMC's Mini and Ford's Anglia 105E burst on to the scene, changing the motorsport landscape forever.

Post-war motorsport mostly consisted of amateur enthusiasts, who drove their cars to and from the circuit. (Author)

IT GETS SERIOUS

With the advent of the Group 2 category for 1961, competition regulations now became better known as homologation (see page 26), which meant that 'production' cars took on a whole new interpretation, fast-tracked by factory-assisted 'works' teams, with Lotus (Cortina) and Cooper (Mini) being two of the best known. And the once all-conquering Jaguar Mk2s weren't having it all their own way anymore, first out-cornered by the more agile Mini Coopers, Hillman Imps, Ford Anglias and Ford Cortinas, and now outpaced by the sheer might of big-engined American racing saloons such as the Chevrolet Impala and Ford's Galaxie, Falcon and Mustang.

The 1960s was a wonderful time to compete or simply spectate, helped by the sheer quality of top-flight drivers. As the Grand Prix schedule was nothing like as choc-a-bloc as it is today, it meant the drivers had time on their hands to try other disciplines. So it wasn't unusual to see Formula One heroes compete in a number of races during an event that pitted pros against amateurs. For example, fresh from winning the 1963 F1 World Championship in a Lotus 25, the late, great Jim Clark then scooped the 1964 BRSCC Saloon Car Championship in a Lotus Cortina! Championship sponsors were diverse, to signify the broadening appeal of motorsport, and they weren't simply car-related either – witness Kent Messenger, Wendy Wools, British Airways, Southern Organs and even BBC Radio 1 all wanting to get involved.

For 1966 the Fédération Internationale de l'Automobile (FIA), the motorsport governing body, announced its Group 5 rules for saloon cars. These were a far more lenient set of regs, allowing more freedom for tuning. And the tuners subsequently had a field day. Fuel-injected Anglias and Imps; eight port-headed 124bhp Minis; 150+bhp Vauxhall Vivas; and not forgetting Formula 2-powered 205bhp Lotus Cortinas and Escorts emerged – all fearsome cars that really added to the excitement in the lower rungs of the motorsport pecking order. However, all this came at a cost – financially for the competitors, at least – and so Group 2 was reinstated for 1970. This effort to get back to the basics only lasted for four years before the affordable 'showroom' racing and rallying Group 1 category was introduced for the man in the street. And boy, did this open a can of worms ...

Production saloon car racing was a development of the rising popularity of 'one-make' championships pioneered by Ford with the Escort Mexico Challenge. It all sounded ideal; strictly standard cars, straight from the showroom and still wearing road tyres, were the order of the day, not purely to control costs but also to entice private entrants to venture out in their affordable cars and have a go. Manufacturers, though, immediately saw the 'Win on Sunday, sell on Monday' potential in all of this and ran works-backed teams with specially prepared cars (some of dubious

With their surplus of power and good handling, Jaguar saloons and sports cars dominated in both racing and rallying. (Jaguar)

legality) and top-line professional drivers. The average enthusiast never stood a chance of victory, especially once the homologation game was played.

Even before the cars turned a wheel, race outcomes were being decided in lawyers' offices. Rules were there for interpreting (bending, some said) and what constituted a car as 'standard' could be anything but, due to multiple legal loopholes. Every car is made for sale to a certain specification, with laid-down tolerances as it came off the production line, and these could be *massaged*. For instance, you were not allowed to modify the height of the suspension springs, yet some identical cars sat much lower than others to benefit from improved handling. How come? Adapting a hydraulic workshop lift to 'sit' on the car for a whole week, or else filling the interior with ballast, thus compressing the suspension to the optimum legal height, were both legitimate solutions as (technically) the suspension had not been tampered with! There were so many other ruses too, some still closely guarded secrets to this day.

Front-wheel-drive Minis quickly became legendary giant killers, especially in club racing where they, along with Ford Anglias, could easily be tuned and maintained by the owner. (Ian Wagstaff)

This is what made the 1960s so wonderful: a wide variety of cars fighting it out, led by World F1 champion the late, great Jim Clark. (Ian Wagstaff)

PLAYING THE NUMBERS GAME

Another reason why private entrants had the cards stacked against them was the difficulty in obtaining the right equipment … including the car itself. To qualify for FIA-regulated motorsport, a manufacturer has to build a set number of cars in an allocated time period (it's usually twelve months) and the same goes for any upgrades; this is called 'homologation'. So far, so good, but because carmakers are global they make different variations of models to cater for specific countries' driving conditions. Thus, it hugely opens up what can be construed as 'factory specification'.

Take the Chrysler (Hillman) Avenger GT. This was itself simply a warmed-up Avenger with a fairly mild 75bhp 1.5-litre engine. After mechanical surgery – adding a brace of dual-choke Weber carburettors, a big-valve cylinder head, and a sports exhaust manifold – it became the Avenger Tiger, and was then decidedly hot. Give or take 200 Mk1 Tigers – all four-door – were converted in the factory's competitions department, and a further (approximately) 400 Mk2s growled down the Coventry production line between 1972 and '73. And that apparently was enough to qualify the car for Group 1 motorsport. With the right bits made in the right numbers, the parts could then be used as options on mainstream Avengers, and all that was required to keep the authorities happy was to show an *intent* to fit those parts. Stories of the allegedly same box of cylinder heads being moved around the factory ahead of the motorsport governing inspectors are the stuff of legends, but were never proved. Hence, the competition Group 1 (production class) GT was a tuned Tiger in

The 1970s saw supposedly standard production saloons and one-make racing. A rung down from Group 1 and less costly, it led to close competition. (Gordon Bruce)

all but name and as a result was a multiple winner in racing and rallying. Bizarrely, the Avenger Tiger also won the Championship in 1977 in 1300cc form – even though no such model was ever made!

Similarly, a legal upgrade by Ford gave a useful pep-up for the Capri 3-litre V6. Called the Higher Performance Engine Pack, it was primarily tailored for high-altitude countries to restore engine power – but, of course, it was never an option in the UK. Similar alterations to a car's transmission (five speeds, better racier ratios, limited-slip differentials and so on) and running gear were also permissible, pushing the private entrant even further down towards the back of the grid. Innocent spectators loved the racing nevertheless. Apart from not being able to keep up with the latest technical developments, the average enthusiast couldn't afford to go racing at all at the top level. Ralph Broad, who ran the works-backed Triumph Dolomite Sprints under his Broadspeed team banner, recalled that back in 1974 it cost at least £20,000 to compete; a sum he freely admitted that would probably have paid for a back-of-the-grid Formula One team!

Pure power dominated the Group A race and rally scene of the 1980s; in exess of 300bhp in the case of the Rover SD1 (MagicCarPics)

As Group 1 progressed over the years, the rules were progressively relaxed and, now with a free choice of carburettors being allowed, saw the Triumph Dolomite Sprint produce up to 190bhp – a far cry from its 127bhp showroom level. Small wonder that Group 1 was nicknamed Group 1½ because effectively it became Group 2 racing at a slower, cheaper pace. The last race took place on 3 October 1982, but happily you can still see these classic racers in action in historic racing today, such as at the excellent Silverstone Festival and Goodwood Members meetings. To compensate for the demise of Group 1, Group N was introduced and broadly reverted to what production saloon race and rallying was intended to be. It was also a complete contrast to the new Group A, which ran up to 1990. Group A became one the best saloon series ever, a joyous era where brute power ruled and crowds savoured some titanic tussles between 500bhp Sierra Cosworths, 300bhp Rover SD1s and the brilliant BMW M3. Yet even this series was blighted by controversy and legal fights, meaning the 1983 season wasn't decided until the '84 Championship was well under way. For 1991 a completely new formula was devised and named as Super Touring Cars.

Although the 1990s Super Touring Cars series had less power, they were as fast and enjoyed a far more varied mix of winning cars such as this Volvo estate! (Volvo media)

This at a stroke killed off the Sierra Cosworth because only normally aspirated (that is, non-turbocharged) 2-litre saloons were eligible. Many more front-wheel-drive cars also came into the mix, with new manufacturers joining the fray under the TOCA (Touring Car Association) banner. This Super Touring Cars series started to find its feet by 1993, and even though there was less power (on average 300bhp) at the drivers' disposal, the cars were just as fast and thrilling as the Group A series, and enjoyed a far more varied mix of winning cars. None was more headline-making than the Volvo 850 – because it was an estate car! You can see them all in their period glory once again now, thanks to the Historic Sports Car Club (HSCC) launching the Touring Car Legends series, which caters for popular racers from the 1970s through to the early 1990s. It remains truly gripping stuff!

RALLYING

The rallying scene broadly mirrored tarmac track racing in terms of popular entrants and rule revisions. Big Jaguars again fared well at the time before the revolutionary Mini came along to rewrite the rulebook and dominate the Monte Carlo Rally during the mid-'60s. Audi's all-wheel-drive Quattro broke the mould twenty years later while, for the UK club scene at least, Ford's (pre-MkIII) Cortina and rear-wheel-drive Escorts were practically the default choice for privateers.

Most car enthusiasts know about the annual Monte Carlo Rally as well as our own round-Britain event, best known as the RAC Rally before sponsors Lombard and then (Vauxhall) Network Q supported the event. The RAC Rally started in 1951, albeit initially as a series of driving tests. It wasn't until the 1960s that special 'forest' stages were introduced to rallying; prior to this, it was contested by teams on the public road at night. This quickly became very fast and anti-social, especially when specially deployed 'helpers' acted as driver lookouts to see if a corner or junction was clear of traffic! During the '70s, pure road rallies were phased out to be replaced by special closed-road events. By mid-decade special spectator stages were introduced, some of them in the grounds of stately homes such as Chatsworth House.

This became a particularly memorable time for the sport, but the best was yet to come in the 1980s when Group B was introduced. Basically these bespoke, ground-effect rally supercars were the rally equivalent of Formula 1, possessing four-wheel-drive and fearsome turbocharged engine power. The speeds they were capable of created massive problems for spectator safety. Three people were killed and more than thirty injured early in 1986, and then legendary driver Henri Toivonen and his American co-driver Sergio Cresto died in their Lancia S4 in May. Group B was promptly banned.

However, national rallying in the shape of the British Open Championship lived on. Classic rallying has become hugely popular. The Monte-Carlo Historic Rally is now in its twenty-sixth year, and if anything is even more popular than the normal event for contemporary cars. In the UK, there's another RAC rally, the Roger Albert Clark, which has been active for more than twenty years in honour of the legend who won the RAC in 1972 and 1977 driving Ford Escorts.

There's also a cluster of smaller, lesser-known events run – just like they were back in the old days – by enthusiastic motor clubs.

And the Winner is a ... Moskvich

Believe it or not, but the first winner of a Group 1 Championship was one of the least-likely cars ever to have pounded the tracks: the Russian Moskvich 412 saloon. This was due to the fact that the initial individual racing categories were dictated by the car's showroom price, and this 1500cc, 80bhp saloon, introduced into the UK in 1969, and costing under £600, was literally in a class of its own. It won thirty-two (out of thirty-three) races to scoop two Group 1 championships and was driven both on the road as a daily car and to the tracks on race days – just as Group 1 intended. The Mosky's domination of the 1972 Championship caused a sales peak in 1973, when 3,462 cars were sold – a genuine case of win on Sunday, sell on Monday!

A dour road car but the tough, reliable if brick-like Moskvich saloon was a worthy winner. (Jeff Bloxham)

BIG FUN WITH A MIDGET

BY TERRY GRIMWOOD

Acknowledged 1970s journalist and track tester Terry Grimwood on how he became a racing champion at the first attempt.

After nearly fifty years I can't remember who it was who approached British Leyland with the bright idea of marking the fiftieth anniversary of the MG Midget by competing in the 1975 BRSCC Production Sports Car Championship. Probably *Cars & Car Conversions (Triple C)* editor Paul Davies.

It was, in truth, an audacious proposition, considering 1975 was roughly four years short of that particular anniversary, but no one at BL seemed to notice. Or if they did they didn't care and *Triple C* magazine, where I was then features editor, was gifted a brand new Midget for me to drive in the championship. To put a bit of icing on an already tasty cake, BL dealer Stewart & Ardern generously chipped in a new Austin Princess as a tow car. Thankfully, I had, for the magazine, experienced a fair bit of track testing different racers under the belt by now, which included a V8 Škoda!

Like the Group 1 Saloon series of the time, the BRSCC Prodsports series was divided into three classes defined by retail price – prices so hilariously low by modern standards that I had to double-check my notes to make sure I hadn't got them wrong. So Class A, the top class, had a price range of £2,250 to £4,000 and featured – wait for it – a V12 E-type, a couple of TVR 3000s, a clutch of Morgan V8s, and one or two Lotus Europas. All under £4k, for goodness sake! Class B – £1,400 to £2,250 – embraced mostly TR6s and Morgan Plus 4s, while Class C, with a ceiling of £1,400, was made up entirely of Austin-Healey Sprites and MG Midgets (colloquially known as Spridgets).

Mine was one of the first rubber-bumper jobs, with the 1493cc Spitfire engine rather than the 1275cc A-Series of previous iterations. Certain fellow C-class competitors muttered about the supposed extra

Terry Grimwood in his double-championship-winning MG Midget 1500, which started off in standard road spec. (Jeff Bloxham)

power of the 1500, which, I'm sorry to say, was unjustified as compromises caused by slotting the larger 'alien' unit into the engine bay meant the power output was virtually the same as before. What it did enjoy, however, was more torque and consequently better power delivery, though this advantage was negated – and then some – by the significantly less nimble handling and more understeer due to the increased ride height to bring the bumpers up to meet US specifications.

Modifications were strictly limited, and mostly safety-related: roll cage, safety harness, fire extinguisher, battery cut-out switch. Adjustable dampers were permitted but there were no upgrades available for the standard lever-arm shock absorbers – though we did temporarily fit a conversion kit using Spax adjustables for a feature in the magazine. Although engines could be blueprinted, we kept on winning the class so never got round to it. However, we did take it to SAH in Leighton Buzzard for a rolling road dyno set up.

From the list of permitted tyres we chose the French brand Kleber … that we then shamefully planed down with a Surform to give barely 4mm of tread to sharpen up the handling.

Most of the prep was carried out with the help of distinguished rally driver and engineer Andy Dawson, who was rather unfeeling in his pleasure at being quicker than me during a test session at Snetterton. Well fair enough – we're talking genuine rally *legend* here.

That '75 season was very enjoyable, nibbling around with the other Spridgets at the back of the pack while the big boys fought it out at the front – a battle won, more often than not, by Chris Meek in his Radio Luxembourg 208 Lotus Europa.

If I remember correctly, we won every round bar the two where Geoff Till gave me a masterclass in how fast a 1275cc Sprite could corner, and ended the season winning Class C in both the BRSCC series and the Direct Tapes Northern Championship, making me the first *Triple C* staffer to actually win a racing series. Not that any fellow *Triple C* staffer had actually *competed* in a full racing series before, but hey, I'll take it. Never did it again though. My venture into Formula 750 racing the following year was decidedly inauspicious, largely due to me deciding to prep the car myself; if my abilities as a racing driver can realistically be described as modest, then my abilities as a mechanic can realistically be described as poor, verging on incompetent. Well, at least I tried.

These days I have a rather lovely Series 3 Alfa Romeo Spider and a 350cc Norton Navigator but I look back at my days racing a Midget with affection, and they only cost the best part of £1,000 to compete in ten races.

ALL GOOD SPORTS

There is a wide range of disciplines that appeal to different types of racers, all with a common denominator: competitiveness.

RACES AND OVALS

The simplest category, which is self-explanatory and also the most popular. A race is usually run on a dedicated racing circuit (some more of a challenge and faster than others) for either a set number of laps or time, with grid positions typically allocated by practice and qualifying times. Grids can be made up of a wide variety of different makes of cars or identical models, as in the case of a 'one-make' series, such as TVRs, Caterhams, Mazda MX-5s and even Ford Ka superminis. Oval racing is broadly similar in concept except that, as the name implies, the circuit is oval-shaped with no diversity of corners. Where oval racing can differ is that the fastest racers may start from the back of the grid to make it more entertaining.

RALLY

Rallies are a one-shot sport that require a driver and a co-driver working in unison, tackling a selection of 'stages' driven against the clock. The co-driver really plays an important part, not only navigating but also 'calling out' the terrain to help the driver by way of what's known as 'pace notes'. These are extremely detailed, often made in short-hand, describing not only the route ahead but also the suggested speed the stage may be tackled at. Pace notes are invariably drawn up by individual entrants practising on the route beforehand, although on certain rallies they are prohibited. As even established F1 drivers rarely crack it in rallying (unlike vice-versa), arguably pure rally drivers possess more natural car control skill than anyone else.

Racing is the most popular category, offering a wide variety of choices to suit all cars and pockets. (Ian Wagstaff)

HILL CLIMBS AND SPRINTS

Both are a thrilling mix of circuit and racing against the clock. Hill climbs are uphill tracks and the name of the game is to set the fastest time to the top. A sprint is similar but contested on a flat track. Both usually last for just a mile, with practice sessions dialled in before doing it for real. Hill climbs in particular are extremely competitive, and it's not uncommon to see ex-F1 single-seater cars taking part.

Hill climbing and sprints are raced against the clock rather than competitors but they are as intense. (victoriajanephotography.co.uk)

RALLYCROSS AND AUTOCROSS

These unique mixes of circuit racing and rallying were devised for television, and quickly gained popularity in the wake of the cancelled RAC Rally back in 1967 due to an outbreak of foot and mouth disease that saw horse racing and its TV coverage banned. At its considerable peak, rallycross enjoyed more than 5 million viewers, and it continues to flourish thanks to the FIA World Rallycross Championship launched in 2014. Events comprise of heats before a grand final, and such was the growing stature of rallycross that it led to several carmakers experimenting with four-wheel-drive hybrids, such as the all-wheel-drive Triumph 1300 and 4×4 Capris, before the all-conquering Audi Quattro rewrote the rulebooks in 1980. Autocross is the later spin-off and is deemed a gentler, faster alternative, being run on grass courses. There is also cross country, which is rallycross but for off-road cars.

Rallying is a great choice for two, often run during the night over tough terrain and murky weather! (racmc.org)

TRIALS

Trials are the rallying equivalent of hill climbing, and remain one of the least expensive motorsport genres because they aren't all about outright speed. They're almost as old as the hills they take place on. Instead of acceleration, the accent is on traction to help competitors get as far up the winding hill as possible, while also navigating pylons that, if touched even lightly, result in penalty points. Like rallying, it requires a co-driver, not simply to help navigate, but also to act as useful

Just like rallycross, the less-expensive autocross involves circuit racing twined with rallying. (Paul Davies)

Trials involve tackling a muddy, slippery, hilly field where traction, not power, is vital. (wayne@classicheritagepr.co.uk)

Autotests are the cheapest form of motorsport and can be accomplished in a standard car. (chris@chrispickering.com)

ballast and to provide a physical 'bouncing' effect that can help 'walk' the car onwards. Aside from using normal production cars (rear-engined ones are the most favoured), special spindly trials cars are also popular for the more serious competitors.

AUTOTESTS AND SOLOS

This remains without doubt the cheapest area of motorsport. It couldn't be simpler: a small piece of ground is laid out with cones to create an impromptu track on which competitors have to navigate the hazards against the clock. Although low in speed, this kind of competitive driving requires considerable skill and precision to negotiate the tight route, necessitating U-turns and reversing while at the same time avoiding the pylons so as not to be docked timed penalty points. Solos is a faster alternative but the principles are the same. The real enjoyment of both disciplines lies in the fact that a standard road car can happily compete inexpensively … even if its tyres become a little worn out!

Homologation Explained: Why it's All About the Numbers ...

Homologation is essentially approval of a set of standards by an official authority, and every car must have a set of 'homologation papers'. To comply with motorsport regulations, a specific number of models have to be manufactured to deem it eligible as a 'production' car for a particular category of racing. Here is a very brief description of the rulings, laid down by the RAC motorsport division and the FIA, the governing body established in 1904.

Group 1

At least 5,000 units produced over twelve consecutive months, with touring cars having no less than four seats. Deviations from the road-going spec are strictly policed unless certain auxiliary components (such as five-speed transmissions) were made available as optional extras when the car was new.

Group 2

Similar to Group 1 but with fewer produced: 1,000 cars within a year. Far more extensive modifications allowed, although the essential elements of the car, including standard suspension attachments and configuration, must be retained. Extra equipment, such as modified and multi-valve cylinder heads, and five-speed gearboxes, are allowed if a batch of no fewer than 100 cars are produced.

Group 3

Essentially Group 1 rules apply again here, although this category is aimed at two-seater Grand Touring (GT) cars, of which 1,000 must be made over twelve months.

Group 4

Pretty much a rerun of Group 2 regulations albeit for GT cars, of which 1,000 must be made over twelve months.

Group 5

Very much a freestyle group, this, just as long as the basic shape and silhouette of the car is retained, and the original engine block remains in place, although this can be extensively modified, as can the chassis and suspension. Unlike the other groups, there are no build quotas.

Group A

Groups 1–5 were swept away in 1981 by the FIA and replaced with just two: Group A and Group N. The former was an evolution of the old Group 2 rules, although 5,000 units now had to be made over the year. Engine modifications were pretty strict and outlawed previously homologated optional extras such as cylinder heads and carburettors, although as compensation 'evolution' models were allowed to be homologated if the sufficient 500 models were made (for instance, the Ford Sierra Cosworth RS500).

Group N

As Group 1 began to lose its *raison d'être*, Group N was devised to bring (affordable) production saloon racing back to the enthusiast using largely 'showroom spec' cars with limited modifications, and with an allowance of a 2,500-car production run. However, this quota could drop to just 250 units if the model was being discontinued. So popular did Group N become that when it was proposed to be phased out in 2013 and replaced by Group R, existing cars could be re-homologated to continue. Consequently, in 2015, a new NR4 (to allow four-wheel-drive) class was devised.

How a car was classified for competition depended on how many were made within a year. (Author)

CHEAP AND CHEERFUL

BY PAUL DAVIES

Paul Davies on the golden days of grass roots club motorsport.

It was all different then. My motorsport began with Autocross in the mid-'60s. It was sprint racing on grass; usually with your daily transport. Cars really were 'run what you brung', although the (new then) Mini was a favourite along with the sports cars of the day – Sprite/Midget, TR2 and Healey 3000 before the Players No. 6 (a cigarette company) national championship came along, resulting in purpose-built racers delivered to scrutineering on trailers. Many events were 'closed to club' so all Dad needed was to have an appropriate membership card or, at the most, a speed licence from the RAC (Royal Automobile Club) and a crash helmet.

The formula was simple. A field somewhere – supposed to be 'smooth' but often muddy when it was wet or rutted when it was dry – with a quarter to half mile track marked out. It all started when you, or your dad, arrived at the venue, chucked out the girlfriend/missus, the spare wheel and any other excess weight that could be removed, took off the hub caps, taped over the headlights to prevent broken glass going everywhere, and used a shoe whitener stick to mark your prescribed competition number on the door.

In the early '70s, as editor of *Cars and Car Conversions*, rallying was the natural progression path from club autocross, sprints or driving tests. Through the '60s the Motoring News road rally championship was top echelon of what became 'road rallying'. The events – usually held at night on public roads in the more remote parts of the UK, but best in Central Wales – were navigational (i.e., demon map reading was an essential) and very fast. To 'clean' some sections the top drivers posted helpers at key junctions to wave them through without coming into contact with locals heading home from the pub. Many is the time an irate farmer blocked the road with his tractor.

It was antisocial and had to end. I only did few road rallies. The budget and lack of a proper navigator precluded my efforts – a collision with a dry stone wall and the MG Midget somewhere near Brecon ending any aspirations. Stage rallying on closed to public roads and particularly forest tracks took over. Dad of the day had a tuned car, complete with roll-over cage, engine sump-guard protection, special suspension, big lights and a co-driver, to sally forth onto the special stages where he (or she if it was Mum) was timed to the second. After six, ten, twenty or whatever stages the winning crew was the one to have travelled the total stage distance in the least possible time.

Not many dads raced Morris Marinas. After a year with a (Ford-loaned) Escort Mexico we were gifted a fully prepped 1.3-litre Marina Coupe from British Leyland Special Tuning. If your dad had raced, or rallied, a Marina he would have told you it wasn't much cop. Mid-'70s, if your dad wanted a good, reliable

Paul Davies with his works-sponsored Avenger. The Hillman was very competitive, although was better known for its success on the racing circuits in Group 1. (Paul Davies)

One of the most competitive and popular campaigners in the history of the sport, and these old school Escorts still rank highly in Paul's memory. (Paul Davies)

and almost sporty family car he'd perhaps have gone for a Hillman Avenger GT, or the Tiger model with Weber carburettors. We won a few class awards in national status stage rallies in one before tackling the Big One: the Lombard RAC Rally of Great Britain. That RAC lasted five days including two nights continuous rallying, had seventy-two special stages covering 370 miles on a 2,000-mile route – and somewhere in a forest in North Wales I entered a corner too fast and put the Hillman on its roof!

The RAC was then a round of the World Rally Championship and contested by all the top works teams, but it was also open to the average amateur clubman. To any Brit rally man it was the pinnacle, the nirvana, but Great Britain doesn't have a World Championship round any longer. Why is a sorry tale, but the events in the current WRC seem a mere shadow of the ones back in the '70s.

Nowadays this dad's motor sport involves owning a classic car and taking part in gentle, non-competitive, runs.

But I'm glad I was active during those wonderful years of motorsport.

After the Escort, Davies and the Cars and Car Conversions magazine he edited campaigned a Morris Marina 1.3, which fared better than you'd think. (Paul Davies)

50 RACING CERTS

Here's a half century of classic heroes complete with their potted histories that your dad (or even grandad) might well have competed with when these cars were showroom fresh. By no means does this fast fifty represent the ultimate starting grid; rather it highlights the wide range of makes and models that were competing back then, perhaps also being driven on the road as well as to the events (and hopefully back home!). Best of all, they still make for great fun as well as competitive competition cars in historic motorsport. Who knows, it might entice you to follow in your dad's tyre tracks and have a go yourself in this fastest-growing sector of British motorsport!

1. MGB

Still a favourite, MGBs make excellent inexpensive competition classics. (MG Car Club & GT author)

Still buzzing …

When contemporary, MGBs made formidable race and rally weapons both here and in the US, where one competed in the famous Daytona 24 Hours as late as 1978. The MGB also raced at Le Mans with success between 1963 and 1965, hitting almost 140mph down the famous Mulsanne Straight. But perhaps its biggest success was an outstanding 1-2-3 at the 1965 Brands Hatch Guards 1,000-mile race, followed by victory at Nürburgring the following year in the world's longest motor race, which lasted eighty-four hours. In rallying the MGB won its class in the Monte Carlo Rally. The B is one of the best common-sense classic sports cars you can buy, and they still make fine road and track cars that can be maintained by any competent DIY mechanic.

There were ambitious plans for the MGB during its development, such as V4 engines and an advanced suspension, but instead Abingdon stuck by its tried and tested components.

Winning formula

This MG still makes a great budget competition classic but it does need a lot more speed for success. Apart from supercharging, the best and easiest route is a ready to drop in tuned engine. Two litres is the optimum size for road and track. Rubber bumpers add over 40kg in weight. Overdrive means six ratios and almost as good as a five-speed gearbox. Competition bodyshells are available from British Motor Heritage.

ACJ 234L

2. BMC MINI

Small wonder

While the Mini was never designed for motorsport, its incredible handling quickly caused it to become a legend and the little 'brick on wheels' is still highly competitive in all types of categories. The Cooper set the scene, although major success only came with the arrival of the Cooper S in 1963. A year later this super Cooper won the 1964 European Touring Car Championship along with an historic maiden victory in the Monte Carlo Rally, which it emulated in 1965 and 1967. It was also the moral victor in 1966 when the entire works team (which finished first, second and third) was dubiously excluded, allowing Citroën to take the win! Numerous national race championships followed up to 1980, and the 1275 GT and Minis still make great giant killers in historic motorsport (such as the Goodwood Revival) as well taking part in its own ever popular one-make racing.

Although the Mini was famously excluded from the Monte Carlo Rally on a minor lighting infringement to prevent three victories on the trot, a Lotus Cortina and a Hillman Imp were also similarly disqualified.

You don't need a Cooper S to make a Mini a giant slayer as they are all very tuneable but it helps! (Ian Wagstaff)

Winning formula

Originally the 850 kicked out 39bhp – today 1.4-litre racers now yield 150+bhp and new ways of tuning the venerable A-Series engine continue to sprout. Ever heard of a 16-valve A-Series? Well, it's now possible, care of BMW motorcycle or Rover K-Series cylinder heads that fit after fairly minor re-engineering and kits are available, as are conventional special cross-flow alloy types.

Arguably the most famous Mini of all, the 1964 Monte Carlo winning Cooper S, piloted by the legendary Paddy Hopkirk (Silverstone Classic)

3. TRIUMPH SPITFIRE

High-fliers

Although Triumph's pretty Spitfire was considered a touch too effete as a serious sports car, project Bom (as the car was code-named) made an impact in national and international motorsport both by Triumph and privateers. First blood was drawn in 1964 when one came second in the Welsh Rally, while a special fastback variant campaigned at Le Mans during the mid-1960s, clocking almost 140mph down the famous Mulsanne Straight, and winning its class in 1965. Over the pond, Spitfire was a storming success in its class in SCCA (Sports Car Club of America), racing well into the early '70s. Other notable success include class awards on the RAC Rally, Alpine, Tour de France and Monte Carlo.

Winning formula

Competition engines can muster up to 140bhp but for road use and light competition driving around 90bhp is the best compromise. The 1296cc unit (with eight-port cylinder head) is considered best but the later, lazier (but some regard weaker) '1500' has more torque and can be stretched to 1.6 litres using parts developed in the US. While fitting a six-cylinder TR6 engine is common, an easier swap is to fit the Dolomite or TR7 unit. The biggest bone of contention remains the quirky rear suspension set-up, although various successful upgrades have been devised over the decades.

The Spitfire's success at Le Mans, helped by its streamlined fastback bodywork, evolved into the slippery style of the six-cylinder GT6.

Racing Spitfires did the groundwork for the six-pot GT6. (Author)

4. JAGUAR XJ-S

After the ill fated XJC project, the XJ-S relaunched Jaguar back into the big time, first with the ETC Championship and an equally successful assault as Le Mans, winning in 1988 (Author)

Cat's whiskers

The XJ-S became a more formidable and successful competition car than its ill-fated fast but fragile XJC a decade earlier, even though they were essentially cut from the same XJ saloon cloth. The smaller, lighter XJ-S was properly developed by the TWR (Tom Walkinshaw Racing) team and speed came with reliability and domination of 1984 European Touring Car Championship – twenty-one years after Jaguar scooped the maiden series in 1963. The car's most memorable victory was the 24-Hour race at Spa-Francorchamps, Jaguar's first 24-Hour win since Le Mans in 1957. With TWR concentrating on endurance racing, the XJ-S came to an end but only after success in Australia and New Zealand. For many years the XJ-S has been highly popular in one-make Jaguar racing.

To enable transmission oil coolers to be fitted, the canny Scot Tom Walkinshaw designed a cunning rear valance under-bumper fitting;. It also served as an effective aerodynamic 'spoiler' that was deemed legal.

Winning formula

In Le Mans tune the V12 made 700+bhp, although more realistically over 500bhp is attainable plus later models were fitted with a 6-litre with well over 300bhp in standard tune. The smaller, lighter, more modern AJ6 straight six (said to be Jaguar's best-ever engine according to one specialist) can easily, and quite inexpensively, make more than 300bhp, plus being lighter makes this XJ-S a more agile, sportier handling choice.

This big cat is a popular club racer in one-make Jaguar championships. (MagicCarPics)

5. SUBARU IMPREZA

Oh, so impressive

With Subaru being past masters of all-wheel-drive, this 'crackerjap' was designed with rallying in mind and as a result won a record forty-six major rallies and twelve WRC championships out of an incredible global tally of 162 before the car maker announced a shock withdrawal from the sport. While the Impreza is best known for its dominance in rallying, it also fared quite well in circuit racing, winning the Targa New Zealand three times as well as a class win at the 2011 24 Hours of Nürburgring – the year before it also set the lap record on the famous Nordschleife circuit for a four-door saloon.

Thanks to rallying success the Subaru Impreza became an instant hit on the road. (Manufacturers Archive)

The 22B STI was a 1998 special edition of the WRX STI, fitted with a larger 2.2-litre engine and an appearance based on the WRC-winning rally machine. Subaru only made 424 of them, with only 24 exported.

Winning formula

Imprezas come already highly tuned, with in excess of 300bhp on tap depending on model and year. Much more power can come from conventional turning methods such as uprated heads and camshafts along with larger fuel injectors, turbocharger (or a switch to supercharging) and intercoolers. 'Stroker' kits are available for engine enlargements. Suspension, braking and transmission bias modifications are best carried out only after consulting one of the many Subaru specialists.

Best for rallying, but the Impreza set a lap record at the Nürburgring in 2011. (Manufacturers Archive)

6. ROVER SD1

Executive express

Easily the most successful Rover in motorsport, the SD1 was a formidable race and rally car by the early 1980s, excelling best on circuits, where the V8 could yield well over 300bhp. First, the SD1 won the 1983 British Touring Car Championship, although was subsequently disqualified for technical infringements, causing Rover to pull out of the British series in mid-1984. However, a non 'works' car driven by Andy Rouse did take the title. The next year, the combination of Tom Walkinshaw and Win Percy notched up six wins in the European Touring Car series but missed out on the championship by a whisker. In 1986 Percy clinched the Euro title, but four weeks later was demoted. Thanks to its pure power, the SD1 became a popular racer in Australia but had less success in world rallying, although it did win a Scottish title. Perhaps the Rover's finest hour was when TWR prepared a batch of SD1s for a special TV rally sprint and a certain Nigel Mansell won the day.

Winning formula

The best starting point is the Vitesse as it already delivers just under 200bhp. In the SD1 the V8 was always a 3.5-litre but subsequently over the decades this evergreen engine was enlarged by TVR to as much as 5 litres and 340bhp for its Griffith and Chimaera models, with further conventional and turbocharging tuning possible.

The SD1 was deemed to contravene the BTCC rules because the engine was found to be using certain non-approved Volvo components, which had been fitted accidentally.

That great V8 engine turned the SD1 into a formidable Group A racer. (Ian Wagstaff)

7. SUNBEAM LOTUS AND TI

Greatly underrated

Although it relied on a Lotus Esprit sports car engine, the Sunbeam Lotus found instant success on rally stages rather than circuits, bagging a famous outright victory on the Lombard RAC Rally of Great Britain in 1980 as well taking the old Rootes Group/Chrysler UK/Talbot manufacturer to overall victory in the World Rally Championship – defeating the up and coming dominance of Audi with its Quattro coupé in the process. Other standout victories included a win in Argentina before competitiveness waned as partner company Peugeot concentrated on developing the sizzling 205T16. The Sunbeam Lotus was discontinued by 1982 but by then this small, simple, conventionally designed rear-wheel-drive GTi was a firm favourite on the UK club rally scene.

Winning formula

As the chassis is Avenger based, it's a well-proven set-up that is easy to improve for competition. In standard trim, the Lotus engine kicked out a quoted 150bhp, but this can now be doubled by Lotus specialists, which in rally tune plus packs 210lbft of torque from a 2.5-litre enlargement. The Ti/Tiger engine is good for around 130–150bhp but now tuners commonly opt for a Ford Pinto (RS2000) engine or the later Zetec, both which have better tuning potential.

Sunbeam 100bhp Ti was essentially an old Avenger Tiger in smaller, lighter clothes. Brands Hatch Racing Stables replaced its hard-used Mk2 Ford Escort 1600 Sports with them for tuition work and celebrity races.

The Sunbeam pipped the mould-breaking Quattro to the 1981 rally championship. (Estoril/Race Retro)

8. VAUXHALL FIRENZA AND MAGNUM

IN A FRENZY

Vauxhall's answer to the Capri may not have set the world on fire but was nevertheless a crowd favourite with legend Gerry Marshall at the wheel, where his 'Old Nail' Firenza notched up no fewer than sixty-two outright wins between 1971 and 1975. Further success included top spots in the British Saloon Car Championship with Marshall (third, 1976) and Jeff Allam (fourth, 1977). It took Group 1 (production) honours on the 1974 RAC Rally, and legendary Pentti Airikkala was a class winner on Finland's 1000 Lakes. In international racing, Marshall came a spectacular second in the 1977 Spa 24 Hours in a Magnum. The Repco V8-powered Firenza ('Baby Bertha') dominated the UK's special saloon series, scoring thirty races and two championships in Marshall's hands.

The rare (only 204 made) Firenza HP came with a five-speed ZF gearbox, which, while being the preserve of exotic super cars, was in fact also available as an option on the Bedford CF van!

Vauxhall relied upon the semi-private team DTV to campaign the fast Firenza. (Donington Park)

Winning formula

The 2.3-litre engine is quite a mine of torque-laden power, with tuner Bill Blydenstein extracting 200bhp in 8-valve form and around 240bhp with the Lotus Esprit-derived 16-valve cylinder head fitted. The engine can also be enlarged to a massive 2.6 litres. Inexpensive tuning parts are still readily available, or the Lotus Eclat engine can be fitted as they are basically the same design. Suspension and brakes are simple to upgrade to cope.

The fantastic V-8 powered 'Baby Bertha' special saloon was borne out of 'Big Bertha', V-8 Ventora saloon which was written off in 1974 (MagicCarPics)

9. FORD CAPRI

Still keeping its promise

This Cortina in sports car drag didn't disgrace itself on the track even though it faced the might of more illustrious competition from Alfa Romeo and BMW in the European Touring Car Championship (ETCC). Out of the massive range, it was the V6 models that got all Ford's attention with special Rally Sport versions such as the RS2600 and the RS3100. The Capri found its feet in the German Touring Car Championship before netting two European Touring Car titles in the early 1970s together with a win at the Spa 24 Hours in 1978 together with some plucky attempts at Le Mans. In the UK, Capri netted a string of consecutive British BTCC and Production Saloon championships, including victory in the Willhire 24 Hours, an endurance event for production saloons.

Capris were popular in the fantastic free-for-all Supersaloon series of the 1970s and a special V6 all-wheel-drive version was made by Ford purely for rallycross.

Only V6 Capris were competitive. (Ian Wagstaff)

Winning formula

Capris need big engines, the ultimate being Ford's 450bhp 3.4-litre quad-cam V6, which powered both the coupé and F5000 single-seaters! In full race trim a 3.0 Group 2 engine developed almost 330bhp with later Group '1/2' and, in period, Group A units only 100bhp less. A popular fit now is the 2.9 Cosworth 24V, fitted to Scorpios in the 1990s, which is good for at least 200bhp and with more to come, or Sierra Cosworth turbo power yielding similar power. There is a myriad of chassis and brake improvements, developed from past racing experience.

The Capri was one of the most successful racers during the 1970s and '80s. (Ian Wagstaff)

10. MOSKVICH 412

From Russia with love

This Russian saloon has to be the most unlikeliest championship-winning car of them all! But the Moskvich was a surprisingly competent race and rally winner during the early 1970s after showing unexpected durability in the 1968 London-to-Sydney Marathon, where three put on a good show with one even finishing in the top ten. The Russian's crowning glory came in the 1972 British Saloon Car Championship, where British racer Tony Lanfranchi's road-going 90mph 412 won virtually all its races and set twenty-two lap records in both the Castrol and Britax series. The car's dominance was due to the racing classes being based upon the car's showroom price rather than engine size. And at comfortably under the £600 category the 412 had almost no competition. In the 1973 Avon Motor Tour of Britain, Moskvichs enjoyed a straight 1-2-3 class win, while in rallying their inherent ruggedness resulted in a class win on the tough South Africa event.

Winning formula

The 1.5-litre engine was quite advanced, being an alloy OHC power unit that's said to be of part Opel and part BMW design. Tuning parts are difficult to obtain but conventional tuning methods such as a Weber carburettor, better exhaust and gas-flowed higher compression head upped the ante to around 115bhp during the 1970s.

Apparently it was Tony Lanfranchi's wife Tina who first cottoned on to the Russian's car's hidden potential and approached importer Tatra Motors, who supplied the couple with three cars.

A dour road car, but the tough, reliable (if brick-like) Moskvich saloon was a worthy winner. (Jeff Bloxham)

11. TRIUMPH DOLOMITE SPRINT

A Triumph of development

A year before the Sprint's launch, a prototype snatched an impressive a second in its class in the 1972 Scottish Rally, although this Dolomite, fitted with Triumph's innovative award-winning 16-valve engine, was better suited for racing where it scored an outright victory, two runner-up spots and a third place in the fiercely competitive British Touring Car Championship. There was also a brace of seconds on consecutive Avon Motor Tour of Britain events, plus a tuned Sprint put on a fine show in the 1974 Spa 24 Hours. Weak rear axles rather curtailed such successes in rallying, although the Sprint came good in Group 1 (production) trim in 1975, with a string of good placings in national rallies, and a class win on the RAC before British Leyland turned its attention to the TR7 V8.

Winning formula

What made the Sprint such a formidable racer was its 127bhp 16-valve engine and overdrive, which effectively made for a six-speed gearbox. In showroom racing tune it easily made 165bhp back in 1974 and 215 horses by the end of Group 1. The Sprint's biggest failing on the track were the standard brakes, but these can now be easily improved.

Broadspeed was the only entrant to make good use of the overdrive transmission but, for all his success, Ralph Broad went on record to say that he considered the Dolomite Sprint to be the worst car that he ever developed for motorsport!

Few road cars were as tailor-made for competition as the 16-valve Dolomite Sprint. (Ian Wagstaff)

12. OPEL ASCONA AND MANTA

Opel fruits

Success for Opel's Ascona (saloon) and Manta (coupé) came late in their lives during the 1980s, with the former scooping the 1982 Driver's Championship just when the potent 4WD, turbo rally car era was emerging. A third place on the RAC Rally gave the Ascona its best ever WRC result before the car took the lesser British title in 1984 and 1985 together with three years of dominance in the Irish Tarmac Championship (1984–86). Then the sensational, if short-lived, Manta 400 took over with a 2.4-litre engine and a Cosworth-developed, 16-valve, twin-cam cylinder head for a fuel-injected 144bhp in road trim and up to 275bhp for competition purposes, albeit still best-suited to rallies than racing.

Winning formula

From 1979 to 1988 Opel made the mainstream 110bhp Manta GT/E, which is easily tunable, plus a similar lustier 2.4-litre cylinder block from the Carlton can be utilised. That said, the plain 90bhp 1.8 GTJ that replaced lesser Manta SRs is by far the best of the bunch for modifying as it uses the later engine found in contemporary Astra and Cavaliers, meaning Vauxhall's sizzling 16-valve XE engine (as seen in the Astra GTE, Cavalier, Calibra) can be installed after relatively minor changes.

The Manta 400 is a rare homologation special, less so the milder Manta i200 – in effect a 400, albeit with a normal 2-litre Manta engine with fuel injection.

Opel's Ascona and Manta were rally stars, the bigger Commodore the track kings. (MagicCarPics)

13. CHRYSLER AVENGER

Still a good steed

This most unlikely competition classic was the result of clever homologation by the manufacturer. The racer was based upon the 75bhp Avenger GT but the Tiger spec (dual-choke Webers, big valve cylinder head, a sports exhaust manifold and and special 'export territory' camshaft) found on Brazilian versions raised the ante to 92bhp. The Avenger Tiger was four-door saloon but Tiger kits were also optional on other Avengers such as the two-door GT. And that's how this Hillman saloon became eligible for Group 1 (showroom) racing, which it dominated, winning the British Saloon Car Championship in 1974, '76 and '77, the later in 1.3-litre guise. The Avenger was just as adept in rallying, winning the British Group 1 championship in 1975 and '76 as well as scoring the car's highest international rally placing: fifth in the famously tough 1000 Lakes in 1977.

Winning formula

In racing tune a 'standard' Tiger engine could produce 130–140bhp, which shows the engine's potential, and in reality it wasn't far short of the ill-fated BRM twin-cam project. However, the modern way of tuning an Avenger is to put an alien power unit in, such as the Ford Pinto unit or the later, sparkier Mondeo-sourced Zetec or potent Vauxhall GTE engine.

Ultimate was the BRM Avenger, where the Grand Prix racing team produced a special 16-valve cylinder head. Also the normal 1600cc engine was replaced by an 1800cc version, which was made for the Brazilian Avenger, the Dodge Polara!

Thanks to cunning homologation, the Hillman Avenger was a three-time saloon champ. (MagicCarPics)

14. MORRIS MARINA

A modern Morris Minor

The most unlikely motorsport machine yet, the Marina did record some quite impressive results in both UK and international rallies. In the 1971 RAC Rally, a Special Tuning-prepared Coupé won the 1300cc class before claiming an impressive second on the Cyprus Rally in 1972. The last 'works' fling for the 1.3 Marina (the faster yet less wieldy 1.8 proved far too uncompetitive) came in the 1975 RAC Rally, where it finished fourth in class. Marinas were far more successful in rallying than circuit racing, although a few did try to compete in the 'showroom spec' price-regulated Group 1 production saloon racing in 1972.

Winning formula

The biggest stumbling block is the antiquated suspension set-up that stemmed from the old Morris Minor. Thankfully any Morris Minor specialist should be able to help here. There's always new ways to find more power from the evergreen A-Series engine, such as crossflow cylinder heads, and stretched to 1380cc, it can yield a staggering 150bhp+, as much as a tuned B-Series. Other engine fits include the MGF K-Series and the Rover T-Series units but the engine bay can easily accommodate Ford units and their five-speed transmissions - or the Rover V8.

British Leyland's Special Tuning division even built a special Rover V8-powered Marina for the 1972 World Cup Rally but - predictably - the Morris Minor/MG Midget-derived rear axle couldn't cope with such might.

The staid Morris Marina never quite cut it but still makes a solid classic campaigner. (Paul Davies)

15. VAUXHALL ASTRA GTE

Still astra-nomical

Vauxhall's answer to the Escort never scaled the heights of the Ford, which some put down to two major embarrassing failures on the 1987 RAC Rally when the engines didn't survive water splashes, one causing Le Mans legend Derek Bell to retire almost immediately with a busted unit. But standout performances include the outright rally title in both the Group N (showroom spec) class and (modified) Group A, while the Astra also claimed overall victory on the 1988 Rally of New Zealand, topping this in 1990 when the UK's leading women driver, Louise Aitken-Walker, drove a GTE to victory in the World Ladies Cup. On the race tracks the Astra's sheer speed helped take it to victory in the 1989 BTCC.

Winning formula

Astras make excellent classic competitors and that Cosworth-aided 16-valve engine is dynamite. Standard tune was 156bhp, and in modified trim over 220bhp was the order of the day – up to 300bhp is now spoken about. For Group N, an ECU upgrade chip along with revised fuel timing settings can see over 172bhp or with a camshaft change, say 186bhp and 182lb/ft.

Ex Ferrari F1 driver and five times Le Mans winner Derek Bell came home a creditable twenty-first in the 1988 RAC Rally plus he won the Autoglass [race and rally] Tour the same year in a GTE.

With GTE, Vauxhall finally had a fine base for Group A and N competitions. (Author)

16. FORD MUSTANG

Horse play

Still holding the accolade of being the fastest-selling car ever, Mustangs have competed in just about every type of discipline. Its first scalp was a class win in the 1964 Tour de France (Automobile), while in its native US, after winning the first Trans Am series, Shelby-prepared Mustangs dominated the Sports Car Club of America (SCCA) scene between 1965 and 1967, with the Ford also mopping up the 1968–69 Trans Am series. Outside the US, Mustang was dominant in the Australian Touring Car Championship. In 1964, it made history by scoring the first win by a V8 before the Ford went on to scoop four more on the trot. In the UK, the Mustang's final fling was in 1970, where a Boss 302 failed to net top honours despite eight of eleven race victories. That fell to a Hillman (Sunbeam) Imp!

Winning formula

Surfing the associated websites will give you a better idea of what can be done. Spares are everywhere, while the simple suspension benefits from the Special Handling Package option; also later independent rear suspension can be installed. The V8 still holds great potential – over 400bhp. Installing a five-speed transmission is doable from a later 1983–95 car.

Roy Pierpoint won the 1965 BTCC, against the more agile Lotus Cortinas and Mini Cooper Ss, although most racers preferred the lighter Ford Falcon instead.

Hugely successful globally, Mustang won the 1965 BTCC against Minis and the like. (MagicCarPics)

17. VAUXHALL CHEVETTE

Escort eater!

After proving itself on the race tracks, Vauxhall wanted to make a rally winner and the Chevette HS provided it – even though it was initially outlawed! Vauxhall's motorsport's DTV division, in haste, readied the rally car before the production version that it was supposed to sire rolled off the line. And because the engine specifications differed fundamentally, tuner Bill Blydenstein had to quickly redesign the cylinder heads to comply with International Group 4 regs. But the revised HS and the HSR evolution were winners, scooping no fewer than fourteen international rallies, although ironically never the elusive RAC Rally that was Vauxhall's main objective. What they did achieve was the British Open Championship in 1979, with legend Pentti Airikkala driving, plus the 1980 Irish Tarmac and British National Championships. Vauxhall proved it could beat the Escort!

Winning formula

In HS tune the 16-valve 2.3-litre engine yielded 135bhp and 150bhp in hotter HSR form, with the rally spec a solid 100bhp to the good. Ordinary Chevettes can be made to perform thanks to the basic single-cam 2.3-litre posting up to 200bhp using Blydenstein tuning gear. Another route is to fit an alien power unit such as the later GM Astra XE engine, Ford's potent Pinto unit or even the original 'illegal' Lotus engine!

Vauxhall strangely only made Viva-powered road Chevettes, although Blydenstein fitted a specially enlarged 2.6-litre Victor engine with automatic transmission for Airikkala's wife – with enough torque, it was reported, to climb a house.

It never won the RAC but the Chevette HSR was a 1970s and '80s rally sensation. (MagicCarPics)

18. FORD ANGLIA

Always new angles

Despite tough competition from the Mini, launched the same year, Anglias were instant winners. John Young's Superspeed car was a regular class-topper in the British Saloon Car Championship and in 1966 – nearing the car's production end – John Fitzpatrick became a national champion in his Broadspeed car (Ralph Broad went on to develop the Dolomite Sprint and the ill-starred Jaguar XJC racer) plus Anglias were the class of the field in UK Oval racing. Ford entered four in the 1959 RAC Rally; three didn't finish but Anne Hall was twentieth overall, while an Anglia would take a praiseworthy eighth place on the 1962 event. They also won their class on the Safari in 1960 and '61, and then, in 1963, achieved second overall. The Anglia campaigned successfully in private hands well after the Escort replaced it and remains competitive.

Winning formula

When it comes to modifying, this Ford is an open book. Depending on regulations, the 997cc engine can produce a screaming 115–120bhp and normally 135bhp in 1.3-litre form with a larger more tunable 1500/1600 between 140bhp and 180bhp. Engine swap potential is vast and just about every Ford engine has been installed, from the Lotus twin-cam to Sierra Cosworth units, but the Zetec and Duratec engines have found favour, where up to 240bhp is feasible in the former and 300bhp in the latter.

Installing modern Ford engines is made so much easier as the transmission's bellhousing bolt spacings have remained the same since the 105E's launch back in 1959!

Apart from much circuit success, the Anglia was an unbeatable 'oval' racer. (Ian Wagstaff)

19. PORSCHE 911

Lucky numbers

Sixty years young, charting the 911's huge history in race, rallying, rallycross and hill climbing would fill every page of this book! In short, this blue chip classic struck gold in just about every discipline both at club and international levels. Major success came in 1966 when the 911 won its class at Le Mans. After finishing third in 1965, the Porsche went on to score a memorable Monte Carlo hat-trick in 1968–70, following up in 1978. Other rallies include the Tulip (1967); Geneva (1967); Swedish (1968–70); San Remo (1968); Corsica (1969); Acropolis (1969); and the Arctic (1972). Two decades later, the 911 won the London–Sydney Marathon in 1993, followed by the British Historic Rally Championship in 1997 and 2001–05. On track, class wins at Daytona, Nürburgring, Spa, Targa Florio, Sebring, Le Mans (in 1974) as well as winning the European GT Championship in 1972 and '73 were the most notable, along with the Paris–Dakar Rally in 1986.

Winning formula

With so many 911 permutations and competition categories it's nigh on impossible to go into how to improve a 911; the best route is to speak to a Porsche specialist involved in motorsport. Bear in mind the one-make Porsche championships where standard road cars can also happily compete.

Versatile 'Quick' Vic Elford (a master in racing and rallying) was first at the 1967 84 Hours Marathon de la Route (held around the Nürburgring) in his daily driver 911 – equipped with Sportomatic part-automatic transmission and a tow bar!

Some sixty years on, the 911 remains a winner in modern and classic circles. (Brian Snelson from Hockley, Essex, England, CC A 2.0, via WikimediaCommons)

20. HILLMAN IMP

Sheer Impudence

Always living in the shadows of the legendary Mini, Hillman's Imp was just as competitive in motorsport. Thanks to the design's rear-mounted engine, traction was excellent, making it an ideal rally car, with the model's most famous victory being outright victor on the 1965 Tulip Rally with Rosemary Smith at the helm. Other success included the Motoring News Championship in 1968 and World of Sport (the ITV television sports programme) Rallycross Championship a year later. On the circuits the Imp proved equally formidable, netting the British Saloon Car Championship in 1966 and '67 and the British Touring Car Championship in 1970–72, although by then parent company Chrysler UK had lost interest. However, the Imp still remains an excellent starter classic and excels in production car trials.

Winning formula

The Coventry Climax ('fire pump') engine remains highly tunable and more than 120bhp can be coaxed from the engine, which can be taken out to 1.2 litres. There's still a handful of Imp specialists around offering tuning parts and advice but the trend now is to fit a different modern engine such as Vauxhall or Ford 16v units.

If you ever wondered how quick a circuit racer like this Hillman was when contemporary, a track test by a leading motoring magazine clocked the all-conquering 998cc 115bhp (Group 5 spec) Imp with a 0–60mph time in under nine seconds and maxing to almost 120mph.

Minis made all the headlines but the Hillman Imp was an equally adept giant slayer. (Ian Wagstaff)

21. CHEVROLET CAMARO

Power play

One of the most successful American cars to compete in the UK and Europe, thanks to their power and noise they made a real impact. In Group 2 tune, the Camaro had the top-tier classes all to itself, in part due to its massive wheel arches that allowed 14in rear tyres to stick the Chevrolet to the tarmac like superglue. It took class honours in the 1971 RAC British Saloon Car Championship, and overall spot two years later. The 1976 GP ace James Hunt won the inaugural 1973 Avon Motor Tour of Britain in his showtoom spec car, and former two-wheel ace Stuart Graham was victorious in the famous Silverstone Tourist Trophy both in 1974 and 1975, where the switch to 'showroom' Group 1 regulations hardly made a dent in its reported 450–500bhp power.

Winning formula

In either 5.7- or 7-litre (including the near identical Pontiac Firebird), there remains huge potential for more power (up to 1,400bhp it is claimed for drag racing) if you look to the US for parts, where the Camaro is still a popular road and track car. The suspension can be uprated using Aldan American damper coilover kits, which allow ride height lowering up of up to 2in. This, along with better anti-roll bars, is a good starting point.

This Chevrolet (along with the near identical rebadged Pontiac Firebird) was brought to our attention when three times F1 World Champion Sir Jack Brabham shipped in ten cars, fitted with the optional performance 'Dealer Pack', for a charity race.

Thanks to its prodigious power, the Camaro could trounce the opposition, which resulted in the car being outlawed for '76. (Jeff Bloxham)

22. FORD SIERRA COSWORTH

Ultimate road racer?

The jelly-mould-looking replacement for the Cortina was made into a competition winner after the purpose-built Escort based RS 1700T was canned, and the RS200 supercar – like the rest of the Group B machines – was banned. Sierra Cosworth was one of the circuit stars of the 1980s; 205bhp in road tune, 300bhp for Group A and a rousing 500bhp for the inaugural 1987 World Touring Car Series. Sierras became as legendary as Lotus Cortinas, netting two British Touring Car Championships (BTCC) after some terrific tussles with BMW. The Cossie took the German DTM touring car series by storm, while in Australia, Dick Johnson netted the 1988 and 1989 Australian Touring Car Championships. A hat-trick of British Open Rally titles in 1987–89 suggested that the large, bulbous Sierra was also another formidable Ford, but internationally the Cossie only netted the 1988 Tour de Corse.

Winning formula

The unbeatable Cosworth engine has been reliably tuned for over 700bhp, with 1,000bhp possible. The conventional suspension (2WD or 4WD) is straightforward to uprate but Ford later altered its geometry settings before the 4×4 model successor and some tuners say it specifically benefits track work. The rear suspension geometry in particular can be improved with a special rear beam while coil over damper kits are worthwhile; it depends how much you wish to deviate from standard, so speak to a Cosworth specialist first.

A Sierra first claimed the British Touring Car title in 1985 albeit with a prototype that looked much like our V6-powered XR4i. However, it was actually an American Mercury Merkur (XR4Ti) fitted with a special, yet simpler, 2.3 litre turbocharged Pinto engine kicing out 320bhp that also helped Ford develop the Sierra RS.

Few cars caused such a stir as the launch of the sensational Sierra Cosworth. (Ian Wagstaff)

Tribute continuation competition cars are becoming more common. Three Group A Cosworth racing replicas, sanctioned by racer Andy Rouse Engineering, are legible for historic racing. (Ashton Parrot)

Although fuel-injected and V6-powered, the European 2.8-litre Sierra XR4i never figured in competition, unlike the American Mercury Merkur derivative which gave the Ford its maiden British Touring Car championship. (Author)

23. SPRITES AND MIDGETS

Always big fun

Little brother to the Big Healey, the original 'Frogeye' Sprite enjoyed a much bigger success in motorsport thanks to its nimble size and excellent handling. Almost before the car hit the UK showrooms, the Frogeye scored a memorable 1-2-3 classic win at the American 12 Hours Sebring circuit race, which led to the legendary lightweight sleeker-styled 'Sebring' Sprites. In UK rallying, Sebrings collected a clutch of victories, including the 1959 RAC Rally Championship and runner-up spot in the 1960 RAC rally. The later MG Midget clone went even better in 1961, taking the first two places on the tough RAC before the Mini Cooper S started to steal the show. The little car's final fling was a works entry at the 1968 Le Mans, when a special alloy-bodied fastback came home fifteenth overall, with an all-ladies line-up taking a class win at Sebring in 1970.

Winning formula

Spridgets (a fondly used slang term for Sprites and Midgets) remain very popular as they are great inexpensive classic racers that excel at minor events such as autotests hill climbs, sprints and circuit racing. With an engine related to the Cooper S, the tuning potential is identically extensive. Or another engine can be fitted, with the modern MGF K-Series or Ford Zetec engines being popular pics. Spridgets handle better than the larger MGB and can be easily improved upon.

Actor Steve McQueen raced one and divine intervention may have been partly responsible for the Reverend Rupert Jones being a class winner on the 1963 Monte Carlo rally.

Few classics make a better starter competition car as a simple Spridget. (Adrian Flux insurance)

24. FORD ESCORT MK1

After the Anglia

While the layout was similar to the Anglia, the Escort was in a different league because Ford engineered a (Lotus-powered) Twin Cam from the outset. Success on the 1968 Circuit of Ireland Rally opened the floodgates as far afield as South Africa and Kenya. The European Rally Manufacturers Championship was won two years running (1968–69), but perhaps the Escort's most notable win was by Roger Clark in the 1972 RAC Rally. Domination of the 1970 London–Mexico World Cup Rally led to the introduction of the Escort Mexico and a popular one-make race series a year later (won by Gerry Marshall), as well as further national rally championships. Escorts were track stars from the flag fall; British championship winners in 1968 and '69, with the Twin Cam and the extremely quick conventional Crossflow 145bhp 1300GTs. The TC was superseded by the new 16-valve Cosworth RS1600 (it being the first 16-valve engine to be homologated in saloon racing), which won the prestigious 1974 ETCC, while the Cortina GXL-powered RS2000's crowning glory was a walkover in the 1974 and 1975 Avon Motor Tour of Britain events.

Winning formula

Engines range from 1.3 to 2 litres but for the majority of historic competitors, interest now lies in the ubiquitous Pinto engine, which can be taken to 2.3 litres and up to 200bhp, although it's also popular to install the modern Zetec/ Duratec Ford engines and, of course, the YB turbocharged Cosworth unit. There are no shortage of transmission and chassis upgrades, but even though most 'tweaks' are now well known, it's still best to first speak to an Escort expert detailing what type of competition you envisage.

Although you couldn't buy one, Ford 'offered' the RS1300 for sale in 1973. In full race tune it produced an astonishing 190bhp!

One of motorsport's lasting legends, original hot Escorts are still front runners. (Estoril/Race Retro)

25. ALFA ROMEO GIULIA/GTV

Latin legend

With such a rich (for its time) standard specification, which included a twin-cam engine, twin Weber carburettors, all-round disc brakes and a low-geared five-speed gearbox, the untapped potency of the Alfa (105/115) Giulia and GTV was there for all to see. No wonder the Italian dominated its classes in the European Touring Car Championship in 1966, '67, '69, '71 and '72, as well as the 1967 European Hill Climb Championship. In the United States, the (Evo) GTA was a consistent winner in its SCCA (Sports Car Club of America) categories, taking the inaugural Trans-Am 2-litre class in 1966. Apart from the Italian Rally Championship and Alpine Rally victories during mid-1960s, the Alfa was more suited to circuits, racking up over 200 victories globally. Today, whether in saloon or GTV guises, they are doughty campaigners in historic racing, especially in dedicated Alfa Romeo championships run by the owners' club.

Winning formula

In their day, Autodelta's wonderful twin-cam Alfa engines could serve up impressive power; 160bhp from the 1300 Junior to more than 200bhp in the case of the 2-litre and modern tuning and tweaking means that these figures are attainable from normal single-plug engines. However, the most popular tuning method is to fit either the 1750 or 2000 engine as a starting point. Despite their age, these Alfas remain pretty specialist and you need a good GT expert to get the best of out of one, particularly the suspension and brakes.

Much of the car's credit has to be put down to Carlo Chitty. His Autodelta tuning company's iconic GTA was one of the first 'Evos' and featured special twin spark plug per cylinder alloy cylinder heads and lightweight alloy body panels.

Most folk lean towards the GTV but the identical if brick-like boxy Giulia saloons are equally competitive! (Author)

26. AUDI QUATTRO

Four-wheel-drive thrills

Audi's Quattro rewrote the rally rulebooks by triggering the four-wheel-drive era. The first win was the 1981 Austrian Janner Rally, followed by its first WRC victory on the Swedish Rally before becoming twice World Manufacturers title winner (1982–83) and twice WRC driver's championship winner (1983–84), as well as taking numerous global glories. Audi also became conqueror of Pikes Peak hill climb, winning three times in succession before, in 1998, switching to saloon circuit racing with the 90 and 200 Quattros in America. In 1990–91 the mighty V8 Quattro dominated the German Touring Car Championship (DTM) – ditto the smaller A4 Quattro in the Super Touring Cars (production-based) series, while the A4 hit the ground running at the UK's Super Touring championship, grabbing top honours in 1996.

The Quattro's mould-breaking four-wheel-drive system stemmed from the 1977 VW-badged Iltis 4×4 military vehicle, which Audi experimented with in an 80 saloon.

The car changed the face of rallying, but Quattro saloons also enjoyed much success (Manufacturer's Archive)

Winning formula

'UR' Quattro posted 200bhp and 210bhp for the 'MB'. Rally engines doubled this, while the V8 A4 racer packed 460bhp, a tad more than the sensational SWB Sport Quattro. Tuning parts from Germany are in abundance but it's not so much pure power that's needed but to fine tune the chassis, not only suspension-wise but also hybrid differentials, and this makes it essential to talk to a known Quattro specialist first.

Utilising a permanent 4WD transmission from a Volkswagen military vehicle, Audi's Quattro rewrote the rally rulebooks care of its added grip and traction, and yet also proved its worth on smooth dry conditions in circuit racing with the 90 and 200 Quattro saloons (Manufacturer's Archive)

27. VOLKSWAGEN BEETLE

Bitten by the bug

As a competition car few are as unassuming as Volkswagen's Beetle. Fast it wasn't, but being the father of the Porsche 911, it too had all the weight behind the driving wheels for maximum traction. Add the VW's legendary reputation for toughness and dependability and a perfect rally car lurked. Its first major success was a class win on the 'Coronation Safari' of 1953, becoming outright winner the following year, which it emulated twice more. By 1972, a competition Beetle could pack nigh on 130bhp from a 1599cc engine, but it was small beer compared to the likes of an Escort or Lancia Fulvia, and a fifth place on the 1973 Acropolis was the bug's final international placing. However the legendary VW continued to shine in minor categories such as autocross and production car trials. And it still does.

Winning formula

Like Herbie, Beetles are still full of surprises, such as the basic engine which can be maxed to 2.3-litres for something like a lusty 160bhp. Other engines can be fitted such as Porsche units or, much cheaper, Subaru power plants. A Porsche five-speed 915 'transaxle' does fit but needs the later IRS rear suspension. The 1302/1303 Beetles from the 1970s used a front strut suspension that found its way (along with the brakes) on to Porsche's 924 and 944.

Continuing the 'Love Bug' Herbie theme, a Porsche 356-engined Beetle was actually made for filming high-speed track scenes.

Today the evergreen Beetle is best suited to trials, where traction is everything. (MagicCarPics)

28. LANCIA DELTA AND INTEGRALE

Bellissimo

Unlike the majority of the other forty-nine sporting heroes, Lancia developed its Delta and Integrale purely for rallying. Based upon the Delta hatchback (a sort of grown-up Alfasud that was Car of the Year for 1980), Lancia added four-wheel-drive to the top model Delta HF Turbo of 1984–85 to make one of the very best hot hatchbacks of its generation, care of the engine's size upping from 1.6 to 2.0 litres, for a sprightly 165bhp in production trim and the 300bhp in rally tune. Lancia took the fight to Audi and steamrollered the opposition to net the thick end of fifty global rallies. Despite its clever 4WD transmission, complete with torque splitting and viscous central differential, the Delta/Integrale never shone as brightly on smooth, grippy circuits, although they have become an occasional sight in hill climbing and sprints.

Winning formula

The HF 4WD of gave way to the Integrale 8v (eight valve) in 1988, with an extra 20bhp, and the following year four valves per cylinder hiked the power to 200bhp. 'Evolution 1' and 'Evo 2' models of 1991 and 1992 upped the ante to 215bhp, while rally car output far exceeded 450bhp and now 700+bhp is even spoken of. Chassis improvements involve larger brakes and lower ride height but seek expert advice as the all-wheel-drive geometry set-up is highly critical; ditto the choice of tyres.

A special two-door convertible was specially made for Fiat boss Gianni Agnelli and is now a museum piece. An Evo III was proposed with a special violet paint finish and was dubbed Viola but – thankfully – was never built.

A modern icon, but don't overlook the impressive Delta-badged forerunners. (Albmartiniracing at Italian Wikipedia, CCA SA 3.0 via WikimediaCommons)

29. BIG HEALEYS

Austin Powers

Austin's Healey is always remembered for its success in motorsport, even though it never really enjoyed one 'big moment'. The 100 competed in most of the prestigious events of the early 1950s but the closest it came to winning was at Sebring in 1954 when victory was on the cards for the new 100S (S for Sebring) before engine problems dropped it back to third place. But the Healey 100 made a name for itself in speed records, with a supercharged specially streamlined 100S clocking 192.74mph. The Big Healey scored much better with outfight victories in the Liège-Rome-Liège, Alpine, and Spa-Sofia-Liège rallies, as well as four top three placings on the RAC event.

Winning formula

The Healey lives on with one of the best-supported specialist and spares set-ups both sides of the pond, and many Healey employees became respected specialists in their own right. Competition potential is considerable, with anything from special chassis and bodies to lightweight 250bhp aluminium engines, either to period 'works' spec or modern interpretations to cater for club level or FIA-regulated events. The rarer four-cylinder 100/4 needs a more sympathetic approach so not to irreparably alter the car and many keep to the Healey-devised M or S spec tunes as a result. Only the 3000 was fitted with front disc brakes.

Before the 3000, some 100/6 'specials' were built, such as the 100/6 S, of which fifty cars sported 3000 disc brakes, along with a higher-tuned 2.6-litre engine fitted to homologate the car for racing purposes

Hugely popular in classic motorsport, the 'Hairy Healey' is a British beefcake. (MagicCarPics)

30. PORSCHE 924/944/928

Putting on a good front

Whether or not the 924 can be now regarded worthy of the badge remains debatable, but the first front-engined Porsche became an impressive track tool once it was turbocharged, raising its VW LT van engine from 125bhp to 170bhp. Not that the near-standard car disgraced itself, finishing twentieth overall in the Monte Carlo Rally and eighth in the Australian Repco Rally. The now highly collectible 310bhp Carrera GT evolution finished sixth, twelfth and thirteenth at the 1980 Le Mans. The 924 was the mainstay of Porsche GB's racing efforts, with a Group 4 car winning the Brands Hatch Six Hours race in 1978. This resulted in a budget-price British 924 series for near-standard (150bhp) cars that evolved into a hugely popular family of Porsche one-make championships, that spouted the popular 944 Turbo Cup race series during the mid-1980s. Since 2021, the 924 has been superseded in favour of the later more powerful models and the Porsche Club GB integrated all 944 models, while in Australia the 944 Challenge Series marked its quarter of a century in 2024.

Winning formula

Uprating a 924 is not easy. Specialists suggest it's more advisable to start with the Porsche-powered 924S but even so around 140bhp was achievable from the fuel-injected Audi/VW engine. As standard 944s posted between 163 and 250bhp depending upon model, engine size and year, well over 330bhp is reliably attainable – with potentially more than 600bhp on the cards! Regarding chassis improvements, it depends on whether or not the aim is to comply with Porsche GB racing regs because there's a myriad of general upgrades around. Consult those in the know, such as renowned Porches specialists, first.

Despite having up to 350bhp in showroom tune and racing at Le Mans (sadly only once with this car still surviving) as well as Daytona, the V8 928 was never a major success on the tracks. Having said that ,Porsche GB still caters for the model and 928s always make good, inexpensive and very powerful muscular track day cars.

Yes you can afford to race a Porsche! Try the 924 and the 944. (MagicCarPics)

31. TOYOTA COROLLA AE86

Flower power ...

One of the biggest-selling cars in the world as well as one of the most mundane, the 1980s Toyota Corolla seemed one of the most unlikeliest motorsport heroes. But the AE86 was something different: a conventional rear-wheel-driver via a live axle resulting in old school oversteer-happy handling. This was all part of the car's success, including a cracker of a 1.6-litre twin-cam engine (which found its way into the original MR2) and an all-in weight of less than less than a ton. The result was an utterly capable, dependable Group A and N racer, netting back-to-back titles in the British Touring Car Championship during the mid-1980s, and beating the likes of BMW M3s, Sierra Cosworths and Rover SD1s. In the European Touring Car Championship, with only 150bhp, it secured the 1986 Manufacturers title. Still a competitive campaigner at club level, the AE86 has also carved a name out in professional drifting.

Winning formula

There are very few standard AE86s around now. The standard engine can yield some 190bhp but it's popular to install other Toyota units such as the 2AZ FE, where 250bhp is on the cards. In its native Japan there are shedloads of chassis and transmission mods together with informative websites.

Such was the distinction of the AE86 name tag that Toyota used it on its great sports car, the GT86. Launched in 2012, it was co-developed and made by Subaru, where their identical car was badged BRZ.

The AE86 moniker turned the humble Corolla into a motorsport legend. (Ian Wagstaff)

32. TRIUMPH TRS

Simply TeRrific

Despite a rudimentary Morgan-like design, Triumph's TR remains one of the most successful post-war competition sports cars. Its first success was outright victory in the 1954 RAC Rally and the TR's toughness and speed soon made the car class of the field, winning most of the British international rallies, including the Circuit of Ireland. Further afield, outright and class wins in international rallies, including Alpine, Monte Carlo, Liège-Rome-Liège, RAC, Tulip and Shell 4000 (Canada), bolstered the TR's CV. However, the sports car was also hot in racing; a factory-prepped TR2 acquitted itself well at the 1954 Le Mans 24 Hours, finishing fifteenth, and was virtually unbeatable in Sports Car Club of America (SCCA) racing. In-house rivalry with the smaller, lighter, nimbler Spitfire saw the TR, even the fuel-injected models, sidelined but today the TR is one of the doyens of the historic motorsport scene, competing in just about every discipline.

Winning formula

TRs are so easy to maintain and uprate, with specialist and club support second to none. The 'wet-lined' engine can easily be enlarged to 2.3 and even 2.7 litres to produce well over 150bhp with tons of torque for rallying. With overdrive available on all forward gears (bar first), it's more useful and usable than a modern five-speed gearbox conversion, argue some TR experts, with overdrive second gear particularly useful for hairpin driving and short spring work. If the chassis frame is sound and 're-bushed', there's no shortage of upgrades; the TR2/3 is most 'chuckable' in terms of handling; and fitting a roll bar notably tightens the chassis frame. Specialists generally say the TR4A, with its independent rear suspension, is better-suited to road tours, although the difference is not enough to consider a conversion.

One 'what might have been' was the '20X' engine: an audacious experimental 155bhp twin-cam unit which won the team prize at the 1961 Le Mans, with all three TRSs finishing. The project was soon culled.

No classic meeting is complete without a Triumph TR joining in the fun. (BlueHussars, CCA SA 4.0 via WikimediaCommons)

33. FORD ESCORT MK2

Simple but successful

One of the most successful and versatile competition cars of all time, the Escort Mk2 remains at the heart of historic motorsport. Continuing on from where the Mk1 left off, the Cosworth-powered RS1800 won its debut rally in 1975, fittingly with Roger Clark at the helm. It went on to win the Lombard RAC Rally a further four years in succession and, in 1979 was the overall World Rally Championship victor, a feat repeated in 1981. The Ford was just as untouchable in the British Rally Championship, with straight victories in 1975–78 and 1980, and continued notching up wins long after the front-wheel-drive Mk3 Escort came on stream. German tuner Zakspeed proved the Escort Mk2 was a force to be reckoned with on circuits and as late as 1982 the RS2000 came runner-up in the Australian Touring Car Championship. Today the Escort is highly sought after in historic motorsport as well as by boy racers of all ages!

Winning formula

Engines range from 1.3 Sport to RS 16-valve but for the majority of historic competitors, interest lies in the ubiquitous Pinto engine, which can be taken to 2.3 litres and up to 200bhp, although it's popular to also fit modern Zetec/Duratec Ford engines and, of course, the YB turbocharged Cosworth unit, all yielding far more than the RS1800's rally tune 275bhp. Depending on regs the tuning potential this Ford is endless with five/six-speed transmissions, exotic multi-link rear suspensions, rear discs brake conversions and more. Specialists and social media forums can provide a wealth of experience and knowledge. Brand-new bodyshells and turnkey conversions are available and the only restrictions is the budget.

Due to revised Australian Group C touring car regulations for 1980, the potent RS2000 racers had to be listed as '2.0 GL' Escorts in race programmes to sidestep any problems.

The Escort Mk2 carried on from the original – and how! Still winning too. (Race Retro)

34. VOLVO AMAZON

Superswede

The saloon that spawned the Saint's shapely P1800 more than sixty years ago, Volvo's (120) Amazon placed sturdiness before style and was a genuine force to be reckoned with in international rallying, competing successfully against upstarts such as the Mini Cooper and Ford's Cortina. The Amazon's finest year was 1963, when it mopped up the European Rally Championship; the Ladies Cup; and, on the race tracks, gave the Jaguar Mk2 a run for its money in the inaugural European Touring Car Championship. Further successes included victory in the Greek Acropolis Rally in 1965 plus third spots both in the tough Safari Rally and the Finnish 1000 Lakes of 1967 although, surprisingly, it failed to complete the arduous 1968 London-Sydney Marathon. Nowadays the Amazon is an accomplished performer in classic rallying.

Winning formula

The Amazon to have is the rare two-door 123GT, complete with a 1.8-litre, 115bhp engine, overdrive gearbox, sports seats, rev counter and sports suspension, but all these and more are available from Amazon specialists. Later Volvo engines, such as the B20, can be fitted easily, as can the unit from the 760 turbo.

Produced until July 1970, a truck-derived V8 looked a potential flagship variant. Reportedly five prototypes were built but the project was sadly shelved.

It was the Amazon, and not the P1800, which showed the Swede's speed. (MagicCarPics)

35. LANCIA FULVIA

Engineering excellence

Before they became reworked Fiats and the ruinous 1980 Beta scandal scuppered sales in the UK, Lancias were loved for their engineering excellence. The Fulvia was a classic case; a delightful overhead camshaft V4 engine, front-wheel-drive and all-round disc brakes provided the ingredients of a classic competition car, and so it proved, with the Italian virtually dominating European rallying for nearly a decade. High points include two consecutive RAC victories, the Portuguese TAP Rally, top three placings in the 1969 San Remo Rally plus victory in the rugged Marathon de la Route the same year. Fulvias commanded the Italian Rally Championship from 1965 to 1973, and in 1972 Lancia snatched the International Championship for Manufacturers, beating parent company Fiat!

Winning formula

Works rally (Variante) HF specials kicked out 130bhp but all engines were quite highly tuned as standard and difficult to improve upon without undue expense. Despite having a singular transverse leaf spring suspension design, modifying is quite straightforward but the brakes (rare Dunlop on early cars) need modifying due to parts availability.

Although campaigned by privateers in endurance racing, netting a creditable class win at Daytona, success on race tracks never got anywhere near the rallying CV. However, an enterprising outfit chopped off the roof of an HF to create a single-seater Barchetta, winning its class in the 1969 Targa Florio as just reward.

The Fulvia was made in the days when Lancia was renowned for its engineering excellence. (MagicCarPics)

36. LOTUS CORTINA

First fast Ford

Fitting a Lotus Elan engine into a humble Cortina Deluxe created one of the stars of the 1960s and the Lotus Cortina remains legendary. In its launch year the LC won the British Saloon Car Championship as well as countless club events, while 1963 (and '65) F1 Word Champion and 1965 Indy 500 winner the late, great Jim Clark also carried off the 1964 title. The iconic red-and-gold-coloured Alan Mann entry took Sir John Whitmore to the 1965 European Touring Car Championship. And when the type's fragility was addressed, the Cortina-Lotus (as it was officially known) won the 1966 RAC Rally, with Jim Clark almost finishing in the top three if he hadn't rolled the car! Such was Clark's presence that later on that the Jim Clark Rally became part of the British Rally Championship. The larger, heavier, Ford-built Mk2 never quite emulated the original's success, although it did win the British Saloon Car Championship in 1968.

Winning formula

The original 1558cc engine posted 105bhp, a period racing unit 140–160bhp if fuel injection was fitted – now around 200bhp is entirely feasible with considerably more durability than before. Many early 'pre-airflow' LCs retain their original Lotus-design coil spring rear suspension to keep it within certain racing regulations and there are stacks of uprating parts available from Lotus specialists, one of the latest being as a five-speed '2000E' gearbox. If originality isn't essential then the plainer, simpler, stronger and considerably cheaper 1498cc Cortina GT makes the better starting point as LC residual values are dictated by the car's authenticity.

Lotus experimented with a full-blown Elan rear suspension set-up. Ford ordered the car to be scrapped ... but it slipped through the net and still survives!

Along with the Cooper S, the Lotus Cortina was the first affordable Q car. (Ian Wagstaff)

The Mk2 wasn't as successful as it was eclipsed by the Lotus-powered Twin Cam Escort. (Manufacturers Archive)

Later LCs used more common, and robust, GT running gear, meaning this mainstream, hotter Cortina could make a better base for tuning. (Author)

37. JAGUAR MK1 AND MK2

Boss Cat

Success with XK sports cars and the big MkVII saloons ensured that the 2.4 would follow suit. It debuted in fine style in the 1956 RAC Rally by winning its class and coming fourth, followed by outright victory in the 88-mile race at Spa. A 3.4-litre engine and disc brakes resulted in more successes, such as a 1-2-3 in the 1958 RAC Rally, while in that year's Monte Carlo just under thirty Mk1s took part, although they had only a second in class to show for it! Future F1 World Champion Mike Hawthorn won the prestigious Silverstone International Trophy and a 3.4-litre also won the 1959 Tulip Rally. The heavier Mk2 hit the ground running and, thanks to a 3.8-litre engine, also dominated the scene with a bevy of famous aces (such as Graham Hill, Jackie Stewart, Jack Brabham and Bruce McLaren) at the helm. One notable race victor was a certain Colin Chapman! Out of the car's many grand slams, the highlight was outright victory in the inaugural 1963 European Touring Car Championship.

Winning formula

Still a very popular campaigner in classic motorsport, the XK engine is now capable of more than 300bhp and of the many developments by Jaguar specialists, modifications include better brakes, five-speed transmissions and even an IRS set-up as fitted to the S-Type and E-Type.

The Mk2 also found fame in record-breaking endurance tests, the most notable being in 1963 when a 3.8 covered 10,000 miles at the Monza test track at an average speed of 106.622mph. After the run it was displayed at the Geneva Motor Show without so much as a wash!

The Jaguar Mk1 was an instant success in both racing and rallying, scoring 1-2-3 in the '58 RAC Rally. (Jaguar)

A bigger 3.8-litre engine with more power and an improved suspension resulted in the Mk2 scooping the inaugural 1963 European Touring Car Championship. (Winspeed Motorsport)

Despite being fitted with the E-type's rear suspension and (with the later 420) a beefier enginge, the heavier S-type offshoot was never cut out for motorsport. (Author)

38. MGA

Capital A

Three aluminium-bodied MGA prototypes (EX182) debuted at the 1955 Le Mans 24 Hours race, coming twelfth and seventeenth. Further successes include worthy finishes in the Mille Migla and America's Sebring 12 Hours, where it ran with the advanced, if fragile, 1600cc twin-cam engine. A further outing with a Twin Cam in 1960 netted a class win at Sebring and twelfth overall at Le Mans. In rallying, the MGA/Twin Cam posted creditable placings on the RAC and Alpine rallies and in 1962 - as a swansong before the MGB took over - Twin Cams scored a first in class at Sebring and sixth in the Tulip Rally. American racers really took to the MGA, winning numerous SCCA (Sports Car Club of America) championships right up to 2005, and this MG remains a firm favourite on the both sides of the Atlantic.

Winning formula

By and large, enthusiasts stick with the conventional B-Series engine, which can easily be tuned in excess of 140bhp, although other engines have been fitted, such as Ford and Mazda engines as well as the modern MGF unit. Alternatively, the MGA can be boosted by 30 per cent by fitting a supercharger - a popular period mod. Don't make the rear suspension too hard, advise MGA experts.

The MGA was the basis of spectacular land speed records, with at one stage, special streamlined, supercharged variants holding almost 100 world records. In 1959 EX181 hit 245mph, making it the fastest MG in history.

Many MG experts believe that the MGA makes a better, more agile racer than the MGB. (MagicCarPics)

39. ŠKODA S100-S130

Just like a Porsche ...

With a configuration not dissimilar to Porsche's 911, it's no surprise to learn that the rear-engined Škodas acquitted themselves superbly in motorsport; especially rallying, where their traction came to the fore, winning their class in the RAC Rally seventeen years on the trot! The coupé 130R (nicknamed 'The Porsche from the East') of 1975 was Škoda's secret weapon, winning the under 1300cc class in the Monte Carlo Rally, followed by a great 1-2 in 1977. Not content with making it in rallying, in 1981 a pair of 130RSs won six out of eight starts to win their class in the highly competitive European Touring Car Championship, beating the might of experienced winners such as BMW and Ford! Four years later, the Group B 130 LR (based on the Estelle saloon) came home fifteenth in its international debut in the 1985 RAC Rally. Apart from making an inexpensive competitive rally car, their rear-engine layout make them excellent for trials and hill climbs due to their superb traction.

Winning formula

Well in excess of 140bhp is attainable from the unbreakable Škoda 1.3-litre engine but VW engines have been installed using special adapter kits for the transmission, although it affects weight distribution. Another tried method is turbocharging. There's no shortage of chassis mods to contain its 911-like handling.

Before Škoda became a low-end car manufacturer during Communist control, the brand, founded by Emil Škoda, was decidedly prestige under the auspices of partners Laurin & Klement.

Czech Škoda won their class in the RAC no fewer than seventeen times on the trot. (MagicCarPics)

40. JAGUAR E-TYPE

Glamour puss

Despite being derived from the racing D-type, by the time the E-type was launched, Jaguar had semi-retired from competition. Nevertheless, Graham Hill won first time out and worldwide success over the decades followed in GT and Modsports racing. A works E-type came fourth at the 1962 Le Mans but, amazingly, this was about as good as it got other than class wins at Sebring on the international stage. There's a difference between merely modified conventional versions and the legendary works-developed alloy-bodied 320bhp 'Lightweights' fastbacks aimed at international racing, of which twelve were made; although fairly successful they only lasted a few seasons. Surprisingly, the lardier S3 V12 was developed into a very successful racer by the American Group 44 racing team for the SCCA production car championships, netting a dozen wins from seventeen entries. Our burgeoning classic scene naturally welcomed the E-type in the Historic Sports Car Club and Jaguar Drivers Club racing series, and they remain a firm favourite at the likes of the Goodwood Revival.

Winning formula

It's a case of how far do you wish to go; the 4.2-litre engine can be taken to 4.5/4.7 litres, dedicated five-speed gearboxes are available and the choice of suspension upgrades (which includes higher-ratio steering racks and electric power steering) are vast. However you need to enlist the experience and knowledge of a good renowned E-type expert to get the best out of any model.

Independent tests just about qualified Jaguar's claim of 150mph but readers weren't informed that test cars were specially doctored, using tuned engines, racing tyres etc, accounting for the extra 10mph that production cars could never muster.

One of the greatest classics, the E-type was also top cat on the track as well. (Ian Wagstaff)

41. ALFASUD

Still bubbly

One of the greatest front-wheel-drive cars of the 1970s, once the two-door, twin-carb Ti (Turismo Internationale) was launched, the souped-up Sud made an excellent competition car. A one-make (Trofeo) Alfasud Championship was devised in 1975, with a similar Alfasud Trophy series quickly spreading to Austria, France and Germany. In the UK, the 1.3 Ti proved no less competitive in the British Saloon Car Championship, netting second in class in 1978 and going one better in 1981 when Alfa diehard privateer Jon Dooley race-readied his tired five-year-old 90,000-mile road car to claim the 1300cc Championship. A Ti even contested the 1980 Hardie-Ferodo 1000 at Bathurst in Australia, finishing a creditable fourth in the up to 1600cc class, while the 'Sud proved excellent at rallying, scooping six class wins in the Monte Carlo Rally from 1979 to 1985. It remains popular in Alfa Romeo owners Club racing.

Winning formula

In standard trim the 1.3 Ti posted a claimed 76bhp but in championship-winning trim the Boxer engine yielded almost double. Later 1.6- and 1.7-litre engines fitted to the 33 can be fitted, although specialists warn the 16V engine is heaver and so upsets the handling, plus the front-wheel handbrake will need changing.

A weird and wonderful twin-engined, four-wheel-drive Alfasud Bimotore 4×4 Wainer was experimented with by Alfa primarily to take part in arduous rallies. Not only did it provide added power and traction, but ingeniously the powertrains also served as 2WD back-ups!

The one-make Trofeo series attracted top drivers, including Grand Prix drivers. (MagicCarPics)

42. DATSUN 240Z

Japan's Big Healey

Regarded as Japan's modern take on the classic Big Healey from Datsun, the immortal 240Z took to rallying like a duck to water thanks to its speed and strength, finishing as high as fifth in the 1971 Monte Carlo Rally. Later that year two top places in Kenya's arduous Safari Rally together with the Welsh International showed the 240Z's potential. In 1973 a second Safari victory suggested that the tougher the terrain, the better the 240Z performed and although the Datsun was a bit on the hefty side for circuit stuff, it became a regular winner in American SCCA racing as well as Australia. In the UK it netted the 1974 Mod Sports Championship together with the 1988 and 1989 Road Sports championships. A feeling of déjà vu after wins in both the 2003 and 2005 East African Safari Classic rallies shows the 240Z has still got it!

Winning formula

As standard, the engine kicked out 150bhp and perhaps 250bhp in competition tune, but now close to 300bhp is possible. And thanks to the Datsun's classic status, there's a wealth of chassis upgrades from Japan and the US. Aside from the normal suspension mods, there are also rear axle conversion kits comprising of contemporary Ford parts, plus rear disc brake conversions.

Spike Anderson's famous Samuri Racing 'Big Sam' racer was such a firm favourite with the crowds that a road-going version was also made available in the mid-1970s.

It looks like a nailed-on racer, yet the tough 240Z excelled best at rallying. (Author)

43. FORD ESCORT (FRONT-WHEEL-DRIVE)

Three of the best?

The new front-wheel-drive Escort didn't emulate the success of the earlier model until a specially homologated Group A XR3-derived RS1600i was announced in 1981. And, unlike the RWD forbearers, the FWD model struggled in rallying, leading Ford to develop the bespoke, mid-engined Group B 'Supercar' RS200. But as a circuit racer the Group A RS1600i – together with its successor, the RS Turbo – did much better, scooping class championships in 1984 and 1986 together with consecutive victories in the 1983 and 1984 Silverstone Tourist Trophy. The Escort reinvented itself in rallying with the sensational 400bhp RS Cosworth, which was essentially the similar Sierra with a high-downforce Escort bodyshell. It scored Ford's first victory in the Monte Carlo Rally for more than four decades, as well as winning the British title before evolving into the WRC rally car. The RS's final victory was scored by Carlos Sainz, father of the current F1 driver of the same name.

Winning formula

In Group A trim the 115bhp 1.6-litre Escort RS1600i delivered 165bhp and approaching 200bhp in full tune; the 132bhp RS Turbo raced with 275bhp and regularly 300bhp during qualifying. The engine can be bored out to 1.9 litres (as per US engines) or more, plus there's a conversion to graft on the later Zetec 2-litre engine block.

Ford was developing a RWD Escort for competition before the Mk3 (FWD) Escort was even launched. The promising RS1700T was a forerunner to both the Sierra RS and the Escort Cosworth but the project was canned in early 1983 after eighteen prototypes were made.

The FWD Escort was best as a racer until the sensational RS Cosworth arrived. (Ian Wagstaff)

44. JAGUAR XK

Jaguar's first sports car

Such was the performance of the legendary XK120 that it immediately acquitted itself to motorsport, attracting luminaries such as Stirling Moss. In its first-ever circuit event at the reinstated Silverstone Tourist Trophy Race, a trio of patriotic red, white and blue XKs lapped the entire field by half distance before finishing one-two. Further success followed, including Le Mans, but rally car NUB 120 is the most famous XK120 of all, dominating the Tulip and Alpine rallies several times as well as collecting a pair of RAC Rally victories before a well-earned retirement in 1953. With more power, disc brakes and rack and pinion steering, the successive XK140 and the E-type-engined XK150S variants were prime movers in classic motorsports from the 1970s and continue to be popular.

Winning formula

More than 300bhp can be extracted from the renowned XK engine (XK150S yields 265bhp), although tuning potential depends on historic competition regulations. When it comes to the handling, specialists advise not to overdo things but stick to tried and tested tweaks, keeping the rear end 'loose'. Stiffer bushes and a geometry check works wonders before fitting dedicated handling packages. A low 4.27:1 axle ratio is ideal for sprints and hill climbs but any mods require better brakes.

Based upon the Jaguar MkV saloon chassis, Jaguar founder William Lyons simply designed the XK sports bodywork as a display exercise for the London Motor Show to showcase his new XK engine.

XKs quickly became the bedrock of the historic motorsport scene. (Jaguar)

45. BMW 3 SERIES

The people's racer?

The 3 Series is most successful touring car in the world. The M3 won the both the European Touring Car Championship and World Touring Car Championship in 1987, plus the German DTM series two years later. BMW says its tally of more than 1,400 global race wins, together with numerous championship titles in almost every conceivable series, right up to world championships, is still growing. In the British Touring Car Championship the 3 Series made history in 2021 by securing an unprecedented sixth consecutive manufacturer's titles, a first in the series' sixty-three-year history. The 3 Series was also one of the first saloon racers to win a significant race, the twenty-four-hour endurance at the Nürburgring, with a diesel (320d) in 1998. On the rallying front, despite championship victories in Belgian and France, the M3 failed to stamp such superiority on the slippery stuff despite a promising World Championship debut win on the Tour of Corsica.

Winning formula

The M3's M10 engine provided the basis for BMW's 1.5-litre turbocharged Formula One engine, which produced a claimed 1,400bhp. Group A racers had 2.3 litres and some 300bhp but its competitiveness lay in its brilliant handling. There's no shortage of tuning equipment and specialists around to help make any 3 Series a competitive historic competition car.

Although the 3 Series didn't set the rallying scene on fire, the E30 holds the honour as the last non-turbo rear-wheel-drive rally car to win a WRC rally.

According to BMW, the E30 M3 has netted over 1,400 wins and still counting. (Ian Wagstaff) Alpina (left) was such a successful BMW turning specialist that the car maker acquired the outfit back in 2022. (Owner Alun Parry)

46. MAZDA MX-5

Modern classic

The world's best-selling sports car has made an equally huge impact on amateur club racing across the globe ever since its 1989 launch, especially in America and its native Japan. However, despite a race series being devised by UK importer MCL in 1991, MX-5 racing was a slow burner until 2003 when owner clubs introduced their own series such as MaX5 Racing and then the Ma5da Racing five years later. The beauty of MX-5 racing is that it's strictly cost-controlled and even caters for standard road-going cars that can be driven to the track. Ready-to-race MX-5s are available in Japan, and while Mazda hasn't instigated a works team as such, an MX-5 competed in the Nürburgring 24 Hours in 2014. Two years later, Mazda UK built a one-off racer to compete in the British GT Championship.

Winning formula

Dubbed 'the new MGB' in the UK, the MX-5 is as easy to own and update and there's a wealth of tuning parts. However, for Mazda competition events any modifications have to be kept in accordance with the relevant racing series rules.

It's well known that Mazda bought a handful of classic Lotus Elans to evaluate and emulate. However, during development, engineers apparently wrote off three Porsche 944s when trying to discover what modern sports car handling was all about!

Affordable one-make racing doesn't come any better than in a Mazda MX-5. (Adrain Flux Insurance)

47. LOTUS SEVEN/CATERHAM

From number six to number one?

If ever a car was ideal for motorsport it's the super Seven, be it Lotus or Caterham badged. Dedicated Seven racing championships have been around for decades, with a factory-sponsored series since 1986, and it's reckoned that there are some twenty championships globally, split between road-legal or dedicated track cars. For beginners, there's the Academy Championship where an all-inclusive package includes the Ford-powered 125bhp car and everything needed to get started. For the more experienced there's more potent machinery such as the Caterham-backed Seven UK, where every (Ford-powered) car is identical. However, any Seven is highly competitive outside racing, such as in sprints, hill climbs and auto testing, and the 750 Motor Club (where this road racer initially cut its teeth) also caters for the car. Plus don't forget that they make excellent non-competitive track day weapons.

Winning formula

While there's an abundance of tuning parts to make a sensational Seven, official race championships are regulated by strict rules, so an entrant needs to decide where and how they wish to compete to become eligible. Race-prepared Sevens are regularly advertised and are usually good value, although they need careful vetting to check their condition.

Such was the Seven's pace that during the 1960s and '70s the car was deemed too fast to race in America and the UK. In 1963 a one-off four-wheel-drive Lotus 'Parkin Cannonball' was built for Autocross.

Super Seven racing is fully backed by the manufacturer Caterham Cars and is furiously fast – and close! (Caterham Cars)

48. VW GOLF GTI

First hot hatch

A racing Golf GTi was built in tandem with the production legend and scored a win at the Hockenheim Grand Prix circuit. In the UK, racer Richard Lloyd set up GTi Engineering in 1977 with support from Volkswagen for the model. Developing his GTi, Lloyd was rewarded with runner-up spot in the British Saloon Car Championship in 1978. Yet despite continued success, he switched to Audi for 1980. Fellow entrants preferred the near-identical Scirocco but a Golf did well in 1982, coming seventh after strong finishes. Internationally, the Mk1 GTi's best result was a class win in the Nürburgring 24 Hours in 1977 but it did better in rallying, winning the 1981 German championship. The crowning glory was outright victory in the 1986 Group A World Rally Championship.

Winning formula

A favourite with tuners since it was launched, the car still holds massive potential via a wide network of VW specialists. Engines can be tuned to 200+bhp, plus later VAG units can also be installed including VR6 and Porsche Cayenne units for much more power – up to 295bhp. Conventional turbo motors (such as the Seat Curpa) have the potential for 400bhp and are a much easier fit.

The GTi wasn't VW having a brainwave – rather it was a small cluster of moonlighting factory engineers who, in their spare time, came up with the right recipe before they showed it to the management. Happily for us they liked what they saw!

One of the greatest hot hatches ever and yet it didn't filter through to motorsport success. (Ian Wagstaff)

49. LOTUS ELAN

Stuff of champions

Although the Elan wasn't designed with motorsport in mind, Lotus soon relented and for 1964 developed the 26R; a lighter, stronger, faster Elan built by subsidiary Lotus Components. And the results flooded in, helped by legendary F1 drivers such as Jim Clark, Jochen Rindt and Jackie Stewart at the helm. In 1965 the 'Comp Elan', as it became known, secured the 1965 and 1966 Autosport Championships. The Elan was equally adept in hill climbing, especially overseas, although true international success eluded the Lotus; the most noble result was Jackie Stewart's class win in 1964 at the Montlhéry GT race. The Scot's special fastback was also due to be raced at Le Mans before it became too badly damaged at the Nürburgring 1,000km. However a French team did field an Elan for its one and only outing at Le Mans. Elans became popular racers in club Modsports and are star attractions at the likes of the Goodwood Revival and Silverstone Festival.

Winning formula

With fuel injection 26Rs could make up to 180bhp but 200bhp is now realistic on carburettors. Racing 26R chassis are still made, but speak to a renowned Elan specialist about the best chassis mods, as some say it is easy to overdo uprating mods, and this includes running on oversized tyres.

In 1972, London dealer Hexagon made a special sports hatch it called 'Elanbulance'; Lotus head Colin Chapman detested it – yet two years later he launched the conceptually similar 2+2 Elite.

Strangely for a Lotus, the Elan was never designed with motorsport in mind. (MagicCarPics)

50. FERRARIS

All thoroughbreds

Ferrari has raced in nearly every touring, sports car and GT category worth knowing and in 2023 won Le Mans – its first since 1965 – after a half century absence by the Maranello Works team. Ferrari made it a clean sweep in the 1972 World Sports Car Championship, winning ten out of the eleven championship rounds, and private teams continued to keep the famous flag flying. Today, the Prancing Horse entertains some of the longest-running one-make championships run by Ferrari Owners clubs (such as Ferrari Club Racing), where grids are made up of all variants, some even driven to the circuit. Apart from racing (up to the era of the 355 Challenge including 308, 328, 348, 355, 456, 550 and Mondial models) there is a dedicated and well-contested hill-climb championship.

Winning formula

Depending upon classification, cars compete in standard or modified form. Utilising a PEP system (Performance Equaliser Percentage) means any Ferrari, irrespective of age, is competitive, says the Ferrari Owners Club (ferrariclubracing.co.uk).

The Ferrari Challenge was devised in 1993 by the manufacturer to soak up unsold 348s. Challenge cars were sold fully equipped with all the necessary safety equipment and a wealth of performance-tuning gear.

Ferraris are not just for circuits, the hill-climbing championship is also well supported. (Ferrari Owners Club)

GOD MADE MAN AND MAN MADE THE CAPRI

BY HOLMAN BLACKBURN

Celebrated racer Holman Blackburn remembers just a tiny part of his love affair with Ford's Capri.

In 1969, having raced a BMC Mini for the last five years and now having the taste for racing abroad, I talked my dad into also selling his Cooper S and putting the money into buying the first of the then new Ford Capri 3000 GTs (in Guards Red).

With Jim Morgan and Jim Rose, who worked for the famous Alan Mann outfit managing the works Escorts among other cars, DPD 9J was ready to contest the 1970 Nürburgring 86 Hour race. And for a 'test day' we entered the Spa 24 Hours prior … Well, it worked – at Spa I finished fourteenth and at the Nürburgring the Capri won its class and finished seventh overall out of 107 entries.

Later that year we were invited to enter the Nürburgring 36 Hours at the famous circuit Nürburgring, which was held in constant rain. We again managed a class win but, more satisfyingly, the fastest lap, which was greeted by a deafening silence by the German crowd at the prize giving – which was better than a cheer. The opposition of 115 cars included a works Porsche 911 and the new competition mid-engined 914/6, yet in the wet they could not get their power down.

I do particularly remember during one three-hour stint at the wheel racing against a silver German Capri 2600. Time and again I would overtake it on the uphill curves but he would surge past on the straights. Later I recognised the pilot as Hans Stuck Jr, who went on to become a Grand Prix driver. Our duel finished as the silver car peeled into the pits, whilst our 26 gallon fuel tank gave us some more miles.

Fast forward to 1980, the 'Silver Dream Machine' Group 1 Capri DPD 9J was, chassis-wise, very similar to the later subsequent Group 1 cars but now with the advantage of Neil Brown engines and special homologation gearboxes.

Ford handed out some special lightweight bodyshells but sadly our little team wasn't on the short list. So we did our own weight saving – so much so that once the car was complete we realised ballast was required – lots! We made inner sill-shaped lead ballast with handles moulded in; one each side just in front of the rear wheels and accessed from the rear inner trim panel, which was held in by bonnet pins as one did not want to play headers with 50kg of lead should a disaster occur!

'Silver dream machine' raced at the Belgium Spa 24 Hours and other European Touring Car races, winning its Group 1 class, and assorted British Saloon car events, never disgracing itself. A truly memorable car, still alive I believe but resting. There have been many other Group 1 and 2 Capris I've had the pleasure of racing but this pair were the best. And it was a great time to go racing too!

Holman Blackburn was one of the most successful Capri racers of the day and still holds a soft spot for the fast Ford. (Darren Garlick/Wikipedia)

One of Holman's Capri rivals was Gordon Spice, who won class honours for six consecutive seasons; 1975 to '82 (Ian Wagstaff)

SEASONAL

PRE-SEASON WINTER WARMERS

Autosport International

Although it's not specifically tailored to the historic motorsport enthusiast, the annual Autosport International, held at the NEC, always throws up enough interest and excitement for classic buffs with its mixture of competition vehicles, anniversaries and celebrities. For the 2024 event Autosport International gained an all-new name – A24 – together with a new look to provide a showcase for anything that races; from the grass roots of karting, to the elite competition of Formula 1. More information at www.autosportinternational.com

The January Autosport show is a great opener to the racing season. (Author)

Many car clubs and specialists exhibit at the show to help wannabe competitors chose the best category for their skill and budget, such as MG racing. (Author)

Race Retro

If you want to find out more about grass roots and club racing, get down to Stoneleigh Park in Warwickshire to visit the annual pre-season Race Retro. Originally called the Historic Motorsport Show, over three days, Race Retro brings together the cars and the stars from the golden days of motorsport. Apart from the wide variety of static displays and motorsport-related trade stands, there's also a live rally stage where aces, past and present, put on a show. Race Retro is a must for anybody contemplating taking up club motorsport. More information at www.raceretro.com.

Apart from the stands and static displays, Race Retro also allows enthusiasts the chance to see classic racers in action. (Race Retro)

Thanks to its wide range of specialists and clubs, for the budding privateer Race Retro has to be the 'go-to' event of the season. (Author)

Almost every year there's something to mark a motorsport occasion. This was the fiftieth anniversary of the 1968 London–Sydney Rally, where a BLMC 1800 almost took overall honours. (Author)

SUMMER SENSATIONS

Silverstone Classic and Festival

The brainchild of popular Group 1 racer Stuart Graham, Silverstone Classic was launched in 1990 as a summer celebration of road and race classics, and has simply become better and better over the years, now regularly attracting attendances in excess of 100,000. The theme for the three-day event (now hosted over the August Bank Holiday) is a unique combination of classic competition cars and classic car clubs on track and in the paddock, supported by a diverse collection of specialist automotive and non-automotive exhibitors. Equally varied are the 'race cards' (organised by the Historic Sports Car Club, or HSCC) which typically include everything from ex-F1 and Le Mans-type endurance racers to historic saloons and GT cars.

Such is the event's popularity that it spawned a number of copycat meetings as well as attracting motor-racing legends and celebrities alike, all wishing to compete and recapture the glory days. Some races are by invitation only. However, what separates the Silverstone Classic from the vast majority of other events is the nightlife. Where others close up for the day, Silverstone comes alive after dark with top bands and performers, and this is a theme others have now copied. More recently, the event has changed its name to the Silverstone Festival to reflect a shift in emphasis. It's no longer simply a competition event but is now a weekend for all the family to enjoy – as anybody who has attended, or even seen the coverage on ITV, will testify. More information at www.silverstone.co.uk.

Apart from the racing, the circuit's fields are packed with owners' clubs and their cars, together with specialists' stands. (Author)

A typically packed saloon car grid thrills the crowd at the Silverstone weekend that's now called the Silverstone Festival. (Silverstone Classic.com)

Goodwood Revival

Probably the UK's best-known historic car event is the fantastic Goodwood Revival, which in 2023 celebrated its twenty-fifth anniversary. This high-octane bonanza was created by the then Earl of March (now Duke of Richmond), who reopened the circuit for racing in 1998 after closure had been forced upon it in 1966 due to safety and noise concerns. Many forget that Goodwood was as prominent as Silverstone in its day. It was also a fast track to be wary of; ending the career of Stirling Moss in 1962 and taking the life of Bruce McLaren eight years later in a testing accident. The Revival was intended to be much more than yet another classic car meeting, but instead an authentic time warp of when the circuit was in regular use. The much-expanded theme continues to this day … so much so that 'the Revival' has become a must-do event even for non-enthusiasts – an Ascot for automobiles!

One of the main attractions is the encouragement to participate in the spirit of the scene by dressing in period clothing. The Revival attracts some of the most exclusive, exquisite and expensive racing cars on the planet, driven by the best and most famous drivers, past and present. Many of these living legends and their careers are also celebrated at the event. For instance, the 2023 meeting honoured Sir Jackie Stewart, who fifty years previously netted his third F1 World Championship title in his final season. And in 2024, there was a tribute to two and four-wheel champ John Surtees, a race solely for Ford Mustangs, and a parage of Beach Buggies to mark both their 60th birthday. All the races (and they are only for pre-1966 cars) are run along the lines they were in period, and entrants are by invitation only. But with so much going on around the circuit and infield, racing forms only one part of the festivities.

Like it or not, over its quarter-of-a-century the Revival has inevitably become more commercialised – and pricier – but each meeting is a sell-out, and nobody comes away less than impressed. If you want more of the same, you can become a member of the Goodwood Road Racing Club and gain access to the periodical Members' Club meetings. These provide similar classic racing to the Revival but the events are not confined to pre-66 machines. More information at www.goodwood.com.

Regardless of the weather, Goodwood provides an unmatched blend of retro racing, with some star names and celebrities taking part, coupled with a unique social scene – the automotive equivalent of Ascot? (Matthew Lamb, CC SA 2.0 via Wikimedia Commons)

It's not just about retro racing cars, other nostalgic vehicles also get a good look in, such as this delightful Comer camper van. (Author)

ROUND-THE-CLOCK FUN

BY REX GREENSLADE

Motoring journalist Rex Greenslade recalls his days driving for factory-backed racing teams.

My racing career started in 1973 when I bought a cheap rudimentary single-seater Mallock U2 Mk 6, which had been a tenth-place car in the hands of the previous owner in the popular affordable 750MC's F1300 championship. However, luckily, the next year Vauxhall found me a drive in a Magnum 2300 Coupé in the Triplex and Britax Production Saloon Car Championships, which was one of many lessons I soon learned: you can't hope to be competitive in such a punishing schedule (thirty races or more) while holding down a full-time job (in my case, being a writer on *Motor* magazine's staff).

The following year (1975) I was part of Samuri Racing's Toyota Celica team in the British Saloon Car Championship, albeit only briefly as I was fired after the British GP round at Silverstone! Alfa Romeo GB and its Dealer Team came to my rescue in 1976 with the fabulous-handling but underpowered Alfasud 1200, again in the British Saloon Car Championship. We got 1300cc engines the next year (1977), with more power and torque, and in 1978 greatly improved the handling and brakes. After the end of the 1978 British Saloon Car Championship at Brands Hatch, the top three drivers in each class were invited to drive the twelve Shell Oils-sponsored Ford Escort Sports, with grid positions determined by pulling a key out of a hat. I drew #12 and thus started last, so decided on the grid to throw any caution to the wind (what did I have to lose?) and was surprised to find myself finish fourth. My prize? Hitachi, who sponsored the race, presented me with a vacuum cleaner (really!) which, as trophies go, sucked in more ways than one.

The following week British Leyland called and offered me the factory 'works' dream drive for 1979 in the championship-winning Triumph Dolomite Sprint – to team up with Gerry Marshall, no less. The season was my most enjoyable, even if, like in 1978, I finished second far too often. But I won twice and took some personal satisfaction in heading Gerry on almost every single time we were on the track. The limitations of the Sprint were only too obvious (especially the brakes), yet the car had been so beautifully sorted over the years that it was an absolute joy to drive.

Throughout 1979, we heard rumours about BL going racing with the Rover SD1 3500 in 1980 and was offered a drive. By that time, I had been promoted to Technical Editor at *Motor*. In addition, I was committed to writing a column for *Motor* each race-day night to be included in that week's issue: often I didn't finish that until the early hours of the following morning, having driven a few hundred miles home from the racetrack. And as I was responsible for all the staff producing road tests, technical articles, new car reviews and so on I felt obligated to turning up on a Monday morning at 8:30 sharp – before any of them arrived. Such a punishing schedule hardly melded well with the life of a full-time race driver so I accepted the invitation (naturally), but only if I was the number two driver.

I have never regretted that decision, even though those that knew thought I was nuts. I couldn't see a life as a professional race driver being a long-term thing. The first year with Rover was great overall but hugely

Dolomite Sprint was now so well developed...

... while the Alfasud was improved over the years.

challenging. I enjoyed the testing, the driving and the racing. There's no doubt that 1980 was one of the best years for saloon car racing in Britain ever. The crowd support was amazing, the cars fantastic and atmosphere intense. By then, however, I was already moving towards my goal of rejoining the motor industry, which I did at the end of 1981, when I accepted a job at Ford. The Rovers had eventually consigned the Capris to history, and as a Ford employee I clearly could only race Fords. This meant I only raced seriously twice more, both the longer-distance TT races at Silverstone: with Richard Longman in an Escort RS1600i (1983 class win) and then Andy Rouse in his Ford-supported American (Sierra) Merkur XR4Ti.

At the time famous Ford's SVE operation was working on developing the iconic Sierra RS Cosworth and my experience with the Merkur provided valuable feedback to the ongoing design and wind tunnel work. Nothing will ever replace the feeling of excitement, trepidation, anxiety and anticipation of being on the grid at the race start but finding other ways to contribute comes a close second. That the Cossie went on to dominate saloon car racing worldwide for years was hugely satisfying, for instance. Perhaps that's the most important lesson learned of all.

The works Rover SD1 season didn't meld well with Rex's day job, but he thought it was one of the best years ever to compete in saloon car racing. (All pictures Greenslade & Bloxham)

THE CLASSIC SCENE

Classic motorsport is on a continual roll because not only is it just as competitive as normal racing and rallying, it's also a lot friendlier and more fun, and gives owning a classic a new dimension. What's stopping you from joining in? It needn't be cost, because with some events you can compete for under £20. And it needn't be the fact that you haven't a competition driving licence either, because more than two thirds of all classic categories don't demand one! Physical disabilities often aren't barriers for competing and many championships happily accept disabled drivers, too. Finally, age isn't a barrier at either end as enthusiasts can start from as young as 14, making it a great adult and children experience – as many do.

The Austin A35 Academy racing has to be one of the most inexpensive, competitive and yet fun-filled ways to go serious racing. (Author)

GETTING STARTED

Walk before you run is a good motto here, so don't instantly think Christian Horner has a Red Bull contract ready for you to sign! You may not want to race anyway – so what about rallying, hill climbing, drag racing …? The list goes on. So, before you decide on what to excel in, attend as many events as you can to get a feel of things. Speak to the competitors for advice, as they are only too willing to help. And while the driving and competing looks easy enough, don't be fooled – because it most certainly isn't! Competition driving is far removed from being on the road, no matter how fast you think you are. Specialist driving schools will help you develop the skills needed and to gain a full-blown competition licence you have to enrol in the approved special race and rally schools to prove that you are good enough to compete – and many won't be. Any driving courses are in addition to essential 'Starter Packs' supplied by Go Motorsport (formerly the Motor Sport Association), then you may have to take an ARDS driving course to satisfy the MSA that you are good enough to compete safely. But if all this sounds too involved, remember that some 70 per cent of classic motorsport activities don't require such licences.

CONDITION COUNTS

It goes without saying that your classic needs to be roadworthy at the very least, but really, given the speed and added strain it will be under, it needs to be in much better condition than simply to MOT standard. Some championships demand that your car is thoroughly checked out by trained scrutineers at each event before it is allowed to compete. If you don't think that you have the skills to keep your car top notch, many marque specialists will prepare and look after your car during the season.

LOOK AFTER YOURSELF

A good many categories allow standard road-going classics to compete while others demand mandatory extras such as a full race safety harness, roll cages and special plumbed-in fire extinguisher systems. For rallying, special 'tripmeters' to gauge distances are essential for navigation, plus you'll also need a brace of mounted stopwatches. Then you'll have to kit yourself out with a quality approved crash helmet and fireproof overalls, gloves and boots – the costs do add up.

TRACK DAYS AND TREASURE HUNTS

You don't have to race or rally to experience the fun: track days and treasure hunts can provide similar thrills. These are non-competitive events, albeit they can provide the same sense of excitement but without the combative competition, expense or even a competition driving licence. Track days have really taken off lately, as it provides a much cheaper way of driving on a track than entering events. A track day allows the driver to drive around the track (usually a well-known circuit) in their own car at their own pace in safety, with or without expert tuition. A treasure hunt or scenic tour have a lot in common with a normal rally but again without the combative nature, although, as with a track day, an element of competitiveness always creeps in! OK, so you may not be the next Lewis Hamilton ... but don't let that stop you having fun competing in your classic!

For those who don't want the expense or effort of competing, more milder pursuits such as treasure hunts may provide just enough satisfaction. In a big saloon, like this charming old Austin Westminster, there's plenty of room for others to become involved. (Author)

One of the many benefits of running an old classic is their simplicity, meaning the owner/entrant can repair or modify the car at the track with only basic tools and equipment. (Author)

750 MOTOR CLUB

Few motor clubs are as proactive as the 750 Motor Club for promoting low-cost motor racing. The outfit, which dates back to 1939 and lists many legendary designers as past members such as Colin Chapman and Gordon Murray, hosts a wide number of racing categories, which for the novice makes for an excellent introduction to the sport. Apart from a clutch of 'Caterham 7' lookalike divisions, there's also Classic Hot Hatch, one-make racing for Renault Clios and Alfas, plus dedicated Mazda MX-5, Toyota MR2 championships. There's also a variety of BMW categories, with even a series for the 1 Series. Visit www.750mc.co.uk

BEST OF BOTH WORLDS

The Avon Motor Tour of Britain

Run during the mid-1970s, the Tour of Britain, sponsored by Avon Tyres and *Motor* magazine, was a brilliant idea. It mixed Group 1 circuit racing and stage rallying over three-day weekends in July and August, and covered 1,000 miles. Attracting some of the biggest names in motorsport, such as Graham Hill, the inaugural 1973 event was won by the late 1976 F1 World Champion James Hunt in a Chevrolet Camaro, which was not too surprising because the Tour was heavily circuit-racing-biased! The following year was far more evenly pitched, and the result was a titanic tussle between rally ace Roger Clark and racing crowd favourite Gerry Marshall in their Ford-prepared Escort RS2000s; the laurels went to the rally legend by the skin of a chrome rear bumper! The auspices boded well for 1975, which saw a 1-2 for rally enthusiasts – RS2000 and Triumph Dolomite Sprint respectively – while in 1976 the highlight was the partnership of James Hunt and Radio 1 DJ Noel Edmonds, although James had other speed-related matters on his mind, for the police were after him after speeding and hitting a tree! Ford Escorts dominated again in 1977, this time with Roger Clark led home by Ari Vatanen. But by now interest in the event, now heavily tipped towards rallying, was waning. An effort to reintroduce the Tour a decade later sadly proved unsuccessful.

The short-lived Tour of Britain was a unique event that mixed circuit racing with stage rallying. (Jeff Bloxham)

IN IT FOR THE LONG HAUL

BY BARRIE CARTER

MG racer and renowned classic car specialist and dealer Barrie Carter recalls the happy-go-lucky early days of affordable circuit racing.

Hill climbs and sprints were the main source of motor racing in the immediate post-war period and it was the norm to drive your car to the meeting, even single-seaters. At a typical club event you simply turned up, stuck tape over the headlamps in the event of them breaking and pumped the tyres up. And if all went well you drove home and used the car as your daily driver during the week.

Then, as Grand Prix teams started to evolve, large factories with elaborate transporters were the order of the day, although the late, great team owner Ken Tyrrell may have been a little more frugal. His F1 transporter – initially for his 500 single-seater and then Minis – was a converted truck which was also used in his business as a timber merchant. I later bought the Cooper Car company's Minivan complete with tow bar, from the legendary John Cooper all for £40. The one you see at shows is not real!

Trailers were not always needed even by top performers, however. Once when Tony Lanfranchi was racing his Merlin sports racer, his tow car broke down on the M1. So, leaving his mechanic to sort it and not wanting to miss the races, he removed the racer from the trailer and drove it to the meeting. He later said that the fines he incurred equated roughly to his prize money that day!

In the 1950s racing teams, such as Jaguar, often drove the works C and D types to continental meetings. Mechanics drove 1950s F1 cars from their town garages to the circuits to warm them up. I couldn't afford a trailer and so drove my own 1275 Mini Cooper 'S' to race meetings, which would have been around 1965 (starting at the Castle Coombe circuit). After driving there from Surrey, I went to the garage next to the circuit and put in two gallons of the best stuff and may also have checked my road-going tyres. However, I owned no racing kit than what I wore and I'm not sure if I even had a crash helmet!

I was one of Jack Brabham's managers at the time and while at my desk I was alerted to an exhaust sound a little different to those emanating from the workshops. I went outside and there was that man Lanfranchi again. He was in the Crosslé and had just driven it off the trailer – or so I thought. Not so, he'd actually driven this out-and-out unsilenced rear-engined open racing car from Belfast no less!

He was stopped by a female copper just outside Liverpool who wanted to check that the speedometer (what speedo?) worked. So she squeezed in and Tony blasted her (this was in the pre-70mph limit days) down the motorway to the next junction and back! He was fined £8, which I paid. I later discovered that the Crosslé had actually been driven to the Nürburgring and back! Happy days.

Barrie Carter has enjoyed considerable success racing MGs, particularly MGAs, for many decades. However now he bemoans the sports' spiralling costs and longs for a return to the good old days. (Barrie Carter)

Carter can count legends such as Jack Brabham, Denny Hulme (1967 F1 World Champion), Ken Tyrrell (Jackie Stewart's car constructor) and John Cooper (of Mini Cooper fame) as both workmates and personal friends. (Barrie Carter)

Cheap thrills? Designed in conjunction with MSVT (MotorSport Vision Track Days), Burton Power's EnduroKA is a campaign of long-distance races where you can compete for £6,000 or less depending on how crappy your Ka is, and enjoy a five-hour race for a further £1,500. (Burton Power)

ACKNOWLEDGEMENTS

A special big thanks for the images in this book goes to MagicCarPics (www.magiccarpics.co.uk), Jeff Bloxham, Silverstone Festival, Race Retro and Goodwood. Valued contributions from Paul Davies, Giles Chapman, Terry Grimwood, Les (Holman) Blackburn, Barrie Carter, Rex Greenslade and Ian Wagstaff, with a special mention to Gordon Bruce. Editorially, my gratitude goes to every car magazine and book that I have had the pleasure to read and digest since 1968, together with motorsport events I have attended, starting with the 1976 British Grand Prix.

Pretty as a picture: a racing two-tone MGB with a matching transporter van to capture that icing-on-the-cake period feel. (Author)

ABOUT THE AUTHOR

Alan Anderson is a well-known and respected motoring journalist and self-confessed petrolhead who has written for virtually all the main car and motorsport magazines since 1983 and edited some ten titles, including *Classic Motoring* and his self-produced book *Go Classics.*